Contents

8

17

18

30

34

43

48

60

COCOON CARDIGAN

Intermediate

SIZES

To fit bust measurement:

XS/S: 28–34"/71–86.5cm, M: 36–38"/91.5–96.5cm

L: 40–42"/101.5–106.5cm, XL: 44–46"/112–117cm

2/3XL: 48–54"/122–137cm, 4/5XL: 56–62"/142–157.5cm

MATERIALS

YARN

Bernat® Roving™, 3½oz/100g balls, each approx 120yd/109m (acrylic, wool) 5

• 9 (10, 11, 12, 13, 14) balls in #00098 Low Tide

NEEDLES

• One pair size 10 (6mm) knitting needles, *or size needed to obtain gauge*

• One pair size 10½ (6.5mm) knitting needles, *or size needed to obtain gauge*

• One size 10 (6mm) circular needle, 40"/101.5cm long, *or size needed to obtain gauge*

NOTIONS

• 2 stitch markers

GAUGE

12 sts and 16 rows = 4"/10cm using size 10½ (6.5mm) needles in St stitch. *TAKE TIME TO CHECK GAUGE.*

WRAP & TURN (W&T)

RS rows: Bring yarn to front of work. Slip next stitch purlwise. Bring yarn to back of work. Slip stitch back onto lefthand needle. Turn.

WS rows: Bring yarn to back of work. Slip next stitch purlwise. Bring yarn to front of work. Slip stitch back onto lefthand needle. Turn.

NOTE

The instructions are written for smallest size. If changes are necessary for larger size(s) the instructions will be written thus ( ). When only one number is given, it applies to all sizes.

BACK

With larger needles, cast on 78 (84-88-94-100-108) sts.

1st row: (RS) K1. *K1. P1. Rep from * to last st. K1.

2nd row: P1. *K1. P1. Rep from * to last st. P1.

3rd row: K1. *P1. K1. Rep from * to last st. K1.

4th row: P1. *P1. K1. Rep from * to last st. P1. These 4 rows form Irish Moss St Pat.

Cont in Irish Moss St Pat until work from beg measures 8½"/21.5cm, ending on a WS row.

Keeping cont of pat, dec 1 st at each end of next row and every following 6th row 5 times more. 66 (72-76-82-88-96) sts.

Cont even in pat until work from beg measures 27 (27-28-28-29-29)"/68.5 (68.5-71-71-73.5-73.5)cm, ending on a WS row.

SHAPE SHOULDERS

Cast off 7 (8-8-9-10-11)sts at beg of next 4 rows, then 8 (8-10-10-10-11) sts at beg of following 2 rows. Cast off rem 22 (24-24-26-28-30) sts.

RIGHT FRONT

With larger needles, cast on 6 sts.

Work 2 rows in Irish Moss St Pat as given for Back.

Cont in pat, cast on 2 sts at beg of next 8 (6-6-5-5-3) RS rows, then cast on 3 sts at beg of following 4 (6-4-4-2-3) RS rows, taking inc sts into pat.

SIZES L, XL, 2/3XL AND 4/5XL ONLY:

Cast on 4 sts at beg of next 2 (3-3-3) RS rows.

SIZES 2/3XL AND 4/5XL ONLY:

Cast on 5 sts at beg of next 2 (3) RS rows.

ALL SIZES

Place marker at beg of last row. 34 (36-38-40-44-48) sts.
Cont even in pat until work from original cast on edge
measures 8½"/21.5cm, ending on a WS row.

SHAPE SIDE

Keeping cont of pat, dec 1 st at end (side seam) of next
RS row and every following 6th row 5 times more.
28 (30-32-34-38-42) sts.
Cont even in pat until work from original cast on edge
measures 17½ (17-17½-17-17½-17½)"/44.5 (43-44.5-
43-44.5-44.5)cm, ending on a WS row.

SHAPE NECK

Keeping cont of pat, dec 1 st at beg of next row
(neck edge) and every following 6th row
5 (5-5-5-7-7) times more. 22 (24-26-28-30-34)
sts Cont even in pat until work from original
cast on edge measures 27 (27-28-28-29-
29)"/68.5 (68.5-71-71-73.5-73.5)cm, ending
on a RS row.

SHAPE SHOULDER

Cast off 7 (8-8-9-10-11) sts at beg of next and
following alt row. Work 1 row even in pat. Cast
off rem 8 (8-10-10-10-12) sts.

LEFT FRONT

With larger needles, cast on 6 sts. Work 3 rows in Irish
Moss St as given for Back.
Cont in pat, cast on 2 sts at beg of next 8 (6-6-5-5-3)
WS rows, then cast on 3 sts at beg of following 4 (6-4-
4-2-3) WS rows, taking inc sts into pat.

SIZES L, XL, 2/3XL AND 4/5XL ONLY:

Cast on 4 sts at beg of next 2 (3-3-3) WS rows.

SIZES 2/3XL AND 4/5XL ONLY:

Cast on 5 sts at beg of next 2 (3) WS rows.

ALL SIZES

Place marker at beg of last row. 34 (36-38-40-44-48) sts.
Cont even in pat until work from original cast on edge measures 8½"/21.5cm, ending on a WS row.

SHAPE SIDE

Keeping cont of pat, dec 1 st at beg of next RS row (side seam) and every following 6th row 5 times more. 28 (30-32-34-38-42) sts.

Cont even in pat until work from original cast on edge measures 17½ (17-17½-17-17½-17½)"/44.5 (43-44.5-43-44.5-44.5)cm, ending on a WS row.

SHAPE NECK

Keeping cont of pat, dec 1 st end of next row (neck edge) and every following 6th row 5 (5-5-5-7-7) times more. 22 (24-26-28-30-34) sts.

Cont even in pat until work from original cast on edge measures 27 (27-28-28-29-29)"/68.5 (68.5-71-71-73.5-73.5)cm, ending on a WS row.

SHAPE SHOULDER

Cast off 7 (8-8-9-10-12) sts at beg of next and following alt row. Work 1 row even in pat. Cast off rem 8 (8-10-10-11-11) sts.

SLEEVES

With smaller needles cast on 42 (42-42-47-47-47) sts.
1st row: (RS) K1. *K1. Sl1P. K1. P2. Rep from * to last st. K1.
2nd row: P1. *K2. P3. Rep from * to last st. P1. Rep last 2 rows Slip St ribbing until work from beg measures 3"/7.5cm, ending on a WS row and inc 0 (0-0-1-1-1) st in center of last row. 42 (42-42-48-48-48) sts.
Change to larger needles.

Proceed in Irish Moss St Pat as given for Back, inc 1 st at each end of following 6th (6th-4th6th-4th-4th) rows to 58 (60-64-66-70-70) sts, taking inc sts into pat.

Cont even in pat until work from beg measures 18½ (18½-18-18-17½-17½)"/47 (47-45.5-45.5-44.5-44.5)cm, ending on a WS row.
Cast off.

FINISHING

Pin pieces to measurements. Cover with a damp cloth, leaving cloth to dry. Sew shoulder seams. Place markers on sides of Fronts and Back 9½ (10-10½-11-11½-11½)"/24 (25.5-26.5-28-29-29)cm down from shoulder seams. Sew in Sleeves between markers. Sew side and sleeve seams.

BOTTOM RIBBING

With circular needle, RS facing and beg at Left Front marker, pick up and knit 32 (34-37-39-44-47) sts down shaped Left Front edge, 78 (84-88-94-99-108) sts across cast on edge of Back and 32 (34-37-39-44-47) sts up shaped edge of Right Front to marker. 142 (152-162-172-187-202) sts.

1st row: (WS) K2. *P3. K2. Rep from * to end of row.

2nd row: P2. *K1. Sl1P. K1. P2. Rep from * to end of row.

Rep last 2 rows until ribbing measures 6"/15cm, ending on a WS row.

Cast off in ribbing.

COLLAR

With circular needle and RS facing, pick up and knit 50 (49-49-47-43-42)sts up Right Front to beg of neck shaping, 32 (32-35-36-39-39) sts up Right Front neck edge, 23 (25-24-26-28-30) sts across back neck edge, 32 (32-35-36-39-39) sts down Left Front neck edge and 50 (49-49-47-43-42) sts down Left Front edge. 187 (187-192-192-192-192)sts.

1st row: (WS) K2. *P3. K2. Rep from * to end of row.

2nd row: P2. *K3. P2. Rep from * to end of row.

Rep last 2 rows 7 times more.

SHAPE SHAWL COLLAR

1st row: (WS) Rib 135 (135-140-140-140-140) sts. W&T. Leave rem sts unworked.

2nd row: Rib 83 (83-88-88-88-88) sts. W&T.

3rd row: Rib to 2 st before previously wrapped st. W&T. Rep last row 13 times more. 55 (55-60-60-60-60) sts rem.

Next row: (WS) Rib to end of row, working sts and loops tog on wrapped sts to prevent "gaps."

Cast off all sts loosely in rib. •

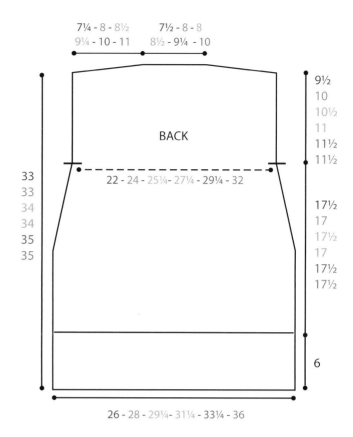

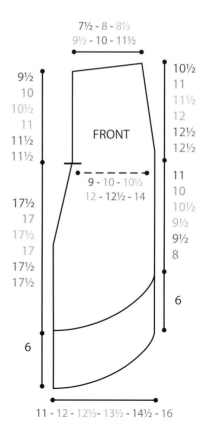

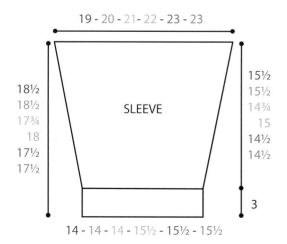

LACE PANEL PONCHO

Basic

MEASUREMENTS

Approx 38"/96.5cm wide x 24"/61cm long.

MATERIALS

YARN

Caron® Simply Soft®, 6 oz/170g balls, each approx 315yd/288m (acrylic) **4**

• 4 balls in #9783 Taupe

NEEDLES

• One size 8 (5mm) circular needle, 36"/91.5cm long, *or size needed to obtain gauge*

GAUGE

16 sts and 26 rows = 4"/10cm using size 8 (5mm) needle in Ridge Stitch pat. *TAKE TIME TO CHECK GAUGE.*

STITCH GLOSSARY

K3psso K3. Pass 3rd stitch on righthand needle over first 2 stitches.

BACK

Cast on 152 sts. Do not join.

Working back and forth across needle in rows, knit 7 rows (garter st), noting 1st row is WS.

Proceed in pat as follows:

1st row: (RS) Knit.

2nd row: K5. Purl to last 5 sts. K5.

3rd and 4th rows: Knit.

These 4 rows form Ridge St pat and 5 garter sts at each end of needle.

Keeping cont of pat, having 5 garter sts at each end of needle, cont even until work from beg measures approx 23"/58.5cm, ending on 3rd row of pat.

Knit 6 rows (garter st). Cast off knitwise (WS).

FRONT

Cast on 152 sts. Do not join.

Working back and forth across needle in rows, knit 7 rows (garter st), noting 1st row is WS.

1st row: (RS) K59. P2. (K1. yo. K1). P2. K2tog. yo. (K2tog) 3 times. (yo. K1) 6 times. (K2tog) 3 times. yo. ssk. P2. (K1. yo. K1). P2. K59. 154 sts.

2nd row: K5. P54. K2. P3. K2. P22. K2. P3. K2. p54. K5. 154 sts.

3rd row: K59. P2. K3psso. P2. K22. P2. K3psso. P2. K59. 152 sts.

4th row: K61. P2. K2. P22. K2. P2. K61. 152 sts.

These 4 rows form Lace Cable Panel at center, Ridge St pat and 5 garter sts at each end of needle.

Keeping cont of pat, rep last 4 rows until work from beg measures approx 23"/58.5cm, ending on 3rd row of Ridge St pat.

Knit 6 rows (garter st). Cast off knitwise.

FINISHING

Pin pieces to measurements. Cover with damp cloth, leaving cloth to dry. Sew Front and Back shoulders along top edge approx 13½"/34.5cm from each edge, leaving 11"/28cm open for neck opening. •

CHILL-CHASER SET

Intermediate

MEASUREMENTS

MITTENS

One size to fit average woman.

COWL

Approx 15"/38cm wide x 59"/150cm around.

MATERIALS

YARN

Bernat® Softee® Chunky™, 3½oz/100g balls, each approx 108yd/99m (acrylic) **6**

Mittens:

• 1 ball in #28630 Pumpkin

Cowl:

• 5 balls in #28630 Pumpkin

NEEDLES

• One pair size 9 (5.5mm) knitting needles, *or size needed to obtain gauge*

• One pair size 10½ (6.5mm) knitting needles, *or size needed to obtain gauge*

• One pair size 11 (8mm) knitting needles, *or size needed to obtain gauge*

NOTION

• Cable needle

GAUGE

13 sts and 16 rows = 4"/10cm using size 10½ (6.5mm) needles in St st. *TAKE TIME TO CHECK GAUGE.*

STITCH GLOSSARY

C6B Slip next 3 stitches onto cable needle and leave at back of work. K3, then K3 from cable needle.

C6F Slip next 3 stitches onto cable needle and leave at front of work. K3, then K3 from cable needle.

CABLE PANEL (WORKED OVER 21 STS) (SEE CHART ON PAGE 11)

1st row: (RS) K6. P2. K2tog. yo. P1. yo. ssk. P2. K6.

2nd row: P6. K2. P2. K1. P2. K2. P6.

3rd row: C6F. P2. yo. ssk. P1. K2tog. yo. P2. C6B.

4th row: As 2nd row.

5th and 6th rows: As 1st and 2nd rows.

7th row: K6. P2. yo. ssk. P1. K2tog. yo. P2. K6.

8th row: As 2nd row.

9th row: C6F. P2. K2tog. yo. P1. yo. ssk. P2. C6B.

10th row: As 2nd row.

11th row: As 7th row.

12th row: (P2. K2) twice. P2. K1. (P2. K2) twice. P2.

13th row: yo. ssk. P2. K6. P1. K6. P2. K2tog. yo.

14th row: P2. K2. P6. K1. P6. K2. P2.

15th row: K2tog. yo. P2. C6B. P1. C6F. P2. yo. ssk.

16th row: As 14th row.

17th and 18th rows: As 13th and 14th rows.

19th row: K2tog. yo. P2. K6. P1. K6. P2. yo. ssk.

20th row: As 14th row.

21st row: yo. ssk. P2. C6B. P1. C6F. P2. K2tog. yo.

22nd row: As 14th row.

23rd row: As 19th row.

24th row: As 12th row.

These 24 rows form Cable Panel pat.

RIGHT MITTEN

**With smaller U.S 9 (5.5 mm) needles, cast on 23 sts.

1st row: (RS) *K1. P1. Rep from * to last st. K1.

2nd row: *P1. K1. Rep from * to last st. P1.

Rep last 2 rows (K1. P1) ribbing for 2½"/6cm, inc 2 sts evenly across last WS row. 25 sts.**

Change to larger (6.5 mm) needles.

1st row: (RS) K2. P10. K13.

2nd row: P13. K1. *P3tog. (K1. P1. K1) all in next st.

Rep from * once more. K1. P2.

3rd row: As 1st row.

4th row: P13. K1. *(K1. P1. K1) all in next st. P3tog.
Rep from * once more. K1. P2.

Last 4 rows form pat.

Work a further 4 rows in pat.

SHAPE THUMB GUSSET

1st row: (RS) Pat across 13 sts. Inc 1 st in each of next
2 sts. Knit to end of row.

2nd and following alt rows: Work even in pat.

3rd row: Pat across 13 sts. Inc 1 st in next st. K2. Inc
1 st in next st. Knit to end of row.

5th row: Pat across 13 sts. Inc 1 st in next st. K4. Inc
1 st in next st. Knit to end of row. 31 sts.

6th row: As 2nd row.

SHAPE THUMB

Next row: (RS) Pat across 21 sts. Turn. Leave rem sts
on a spare needle.

***Next row:** Cast on 1 st. P9 (including cast on st). Turn. Leave rem sts on a spare needle.

Next row: Cast on 1 st. K10 (including cast on st). Work a further 5 rows in stocking st on these 10 sts.

Next row: (RS) (K2tog) 5 times. 5 sts.

Next row: (P2tog) twice. P1. 3 sts. Break yarn, leaving a long end. Draw end tightly through rem sts. Sew thumb seam.

Next row: (RS) Rejoin yarn. Pick up and knit 2 sts over cast on sts at base of thumb. Pat to end of row across sts from spare needle. 25 sts.***

Cont in pat until work from beg measures approx 9½"/24cm, ending with the following pat row:

Last row: (WS) P13. K1. *P3tog. (K1. P1. K1) all in next st. Rep from * once more. K1. P2.

1st row: (RS) K2. P10. ssk. K2tog. K6. ssk. K1. 22 sts.

2nd row: P10. K2. (P3tog. K1) twice. P2. 18 sts.

3rd row: K2tog. (P2tog) 3 times. (K2tog) 5 times. 9 sts.

Break yarn leaving a long end. Draw end tightly through rem sts. Sew side seam.

LEFT MITTEN

Work from ** to ** as given for Right Mitten.

Change to larger (6.5 mm) needles.

1st row: (RS) K13. P10. K2.

2nd row: P2. K1. *P3tog. (K1. P1. K1) all in next st.

Rep from * once more. K1. P13.

3rd row: As 1st row.

4th row: P2. K1. *(K1. P1. K1) all in next st. P3tog. Rep from * once more. K1. P13. Last 4 rows form pat. Work a further 4 rows in pat.

SHAPE THUMB GUSSET

1st row: (RS) Pat across 10 sts. Inc 1 st in each of next 2 sts. Pat to end of row.

2nd and following alt rows: Work even in pat.

3rd row: Pat across 10 sts. Inc 1 st in next st. K2. Inc 1 st in next st. Knit to end of row.

5th row: Pat across 10 sts. Inc 1 st in next st. K4. Inc 1 st in next st. Knit to end of row. 31 sts.

6th row: As 2nd row.

SHAPE THUMB

Next row: (RS) Pat across 18 sts. Turn. Leave rem sts on a spare needle. Work from *** to *** as given for Right Mitten.

Cont in pat until work from beg measures approx 9½"/24cm, ending with the following pat row:

Last row: (WS) P2. K1. *P3tog. (K1. P1. K1) all in next st. Rep from * once more. K1. P13.

SHAPE TOP

1st row: (RS) K1. K2tog. K6. K2tog. ssk. P10. K2. 22 sts.

2nd row: P2. K2. (P3tog. K1) twice. P10. 18 sts.

3rd row: (K2tog) 5 times. (P2tog) 3 times. K2tog. 9 sts. Break yarn, leaving a long end. Draw end tightly through rem sts. Sew side seam.

COWL

With 8 mm needles, cast on 45 sts.

1st row: (RS) K2. P10. Work 1st row of Cable Panel across next 21 sts. P10. K2.

2nd row: K2. *P3tog. (K1. P1. K1) all in next st. Rep from * once more. K2. Work 2nd row of Cable Panel across next 21 sts. K2. **(K1. P1. K1) all in next st. P3tog. Rep from ** once more. K2.

3rd row: K2. P10. Work 3rd row of Cable Panel across next 21 sts. P10. K2.

4th row: K2. *(K1. P1. K1) all in next st. P3tog. Rep from * once more. K2. Work 4th row of Cable Panel across next 21 sts. K2. **P3tog. (K1. P1. K1) all in next st. Rep from ** once more. K2.

These 4 rows form Trinity St pat. Cable Panel is now in position.

Cont in pat, keeping cont of Cable Panel, until work from beg measures approx 59"/150cm ending on a 10th row of Cable Panel pat.

Cast off in pat.

FINISHING

Sew cast on and cast off edges tog. Sew center back seam. •

Chart

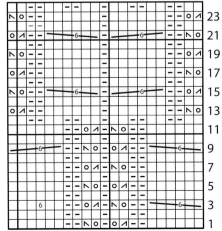

Key

☐ = Knit on RS rows.
Purl on WS rows.
⊟ = Purl on RS rows.
Knit on WS rows.
▥ = C6B
▥ = C6F
⊡ = yo
⊠ = ssk
⊿ = K2tog

Start Here

BATWING SWONCHO

Intermediate

SIZES

To fit bust measurement:

XS/M: 28–38"/71–96.5cm

L/XL: 40–46"/101.5–117cm

2/5XL: 48–62"/122–157.5cm

MATERIALS

YARN

Patons® Classic Wool Worsted™, 3½oz/100g balls, each approx 194yd/177m (wool) **⑤**

• 9 (10, 12) balls in #77791 Cool Gray

NEEDLES

• One pair size 7 (4.5mm) knitting needles, *or size needed to obtain gauge*

• One size 7 (4.5mm) circular needle, 36"/91.5cm long, *or size needed to obtain gauge*

NOTIONS

• 4 stitch holders

• Stitch markers

GAUGE

20 sts and 26 rows = 4"/10cm using size 7 (4.5mm) needles in St st. *TAKE TIME TO CHECK GAUGE.*

LACE PANEL (WORKED OVER 43 STS)

See chart on page 16.

1st row: (RS) *P2. K1tbl. P1. K1tbl. P2. K7. P2. K1tbl. P1. K1tbl. P2.* P1. Rep from * to * once more.

2nd and alt rows to 18th row: Knit all knit sts, purl all purl and yo sts, P1tbl all K1tbl sts as they appear.

3rd row: P2. K1tbl. P1. K1tbl. P2. K6. ssk. (P1. K1tbl) twice. P2. yo. P1. yo. P2. (K1tbl. P1) twice. K2tog. K6. P2. K1tbl. P1. K1tbl. P2.

5th row: P2. K1tbl. P1. K1tbl. P2. K5. ssk. (P1. K1tbl) twice. P2. yo. K1. P1. K1. yo. P2. (K1tbl. P1) twice. K2tog. K5. P2. K1tbl. P1. K1tbl. P2.

7th row: P2. K1tbl. P1. K1tbl. P2. K4. ssk. (P1. K1tbl) twice. P2. yo. K2. P1. K2. yo. P2. (K1tbl. P1) twice. K2tog. K4. P2. K1tbl. P1. K1tbl. P2.

9th row: P2. K1tbl. P1. K1tbl. P2. K3. ssk. (P1. K1tbl) twice. P2. yo. K3. P1. K3. yo. P2. (K1tbl. P1) twice. K2tog. K3. P2. K1tbl. P1. K1tbl. P2.

11th row: P2. K1tbl. P1. K1tbl. P2. K2. ssk. (P1. K1tbl) twice. P2. yo. K4. P1. K4. yo. P2. (K1tbl. P1) twice. K2tog. K2. P2. K1tbl. P1. K1tbl. P2.

13th row: P2. K1tbl. P1. K1tbl. P2. K1. ssk. (P1. K1tbl) twice. P2. yo. K5. P1. K5. yo. P2. (K1tbl. P1) twice. K2tog. K1. P2. K1tbl. P1. K1tbl. P2.

15th row: P2. K1tbl. P1. K1tbl. P2. ssk. (P1. K1tbl) twice. P2. yo. K6. P1. K6. yo. P2. (K1tbl. P1) twice. K2tog. P2. K1tbl. P1. K1tbl. P2.

17th row: *(P2. K1tbl. P1. K1tbl. P2) twice.* K7. P1. K7. Rep from * to * once more.

19th row: P2. K1tbl. P1. K1tbl. P4. (K1tbl. P1) twice. K2tog. K6. yo. P1. yo. K6. ssk. (P1. K1tbl) twice. P4. K1tbl. P1. K1tbl. P2.

20th and alt rows to 32nd row: Knit all knit and yo sts, purl all purl sts, P1tbl all K1tbl sts as they appear.

21st row: P2. K1tbl. P1. K1tbl. P4. K1tbl. P1. K1tbl. K2tog. K6. yo. P3. yo. K6. ssk. K1tbl. P1. K1tbl. P4. K1tbl. P1. K1tbl. P2.

23rd row: P2. K1tbl. P1. K1tbl. P4. K1tbl. P1. K2tog. K6. yo. P5. yo. K6. ssk. P1. K1tbl. P4. K1tbl. P1. K1tbl. P2.

25th row: P2. K1tbl. P1. K1tbl. P4. K1tbl. K2tog. K6. yo. K1tbl. P5. K1tbl. yo. K6. ssk. K1tbl. P4. K1tbl. P1. K1tbl. P2.

27th row: P2. K1tbl. P1. K1tbl. P4. K2tog. K6. yo. P1. K1tbl. P5. K1tbl. P1. yo. K6. ssk. P4. K1tbl. P1. K1tbl. P2.

29th row: P2. K1tbl. P1. K1tbl. P3. K2tog. K6. yo. K1tbl. P1. K1tbl. P5. K1tbl. P1. K1tbl. yo. K6. ssk. P3. K1tbl. P1. K1tbl. P2.

31st row: P2. K1tbl. P1. K1tbl. P2. K2tog. K6. yo. (P1. K1tbl) twice. P5. (K1tbl. P1) twice. yo. K6. ssk. P2. K1tbl. P1. K1tbl. P2.

32nd row: As 20th row.

These 32 rows form Lace Panel Pat.

NOTES

The instructions are written for smallest size. If changes are necessary for larger size(s) the instructions will be written thus ( ). When only one number is given, it applies to all sizes.

BACK

**With pair of needles, cast on 47 (59-71) sts.

1st row: (RS) K2 (8-14). Work 1st row of Lace Panel. K2 (8-14).

2nd row: P2 (8-14). Work 2nd row of Lace Panel. P2 (8-14).

Lace Panel is now in position.

Note: Move to circular needle when necessary to accommodate all sts.

SHAPE SIDES

Keeping cont of pat, cast on 4 sts at beg of next 10 rows, cast on 3 sts at beg of following 10 rows, then inc 1 st each end of needle on next 8 rows, taking inc sts into stocking st. 133 (145-157) sts.

Inc 1 st each end of needle on next and every following alt row 3 times more, taking inc sts into stocking st. 141 (153-165) sts.

Work 2 rows even.

Inc 1 st each end of next and every following 4th row twice more, taking inc sts into stocking st. 147 (159-171) sts. PM at each end of last row.

SHAPE RAGLANS

Keeping cont of pat, proceed as follows:

1st row: (RS) K2. ssk. Pat to last 4 sts. K2tog. K2.

2nd to 4th rows: Work even in pat.

Rep last 4 rows 23 (22-21) times more. 99 (113-127) sts. Proceed as follows:

1st row: (RS) K2. ssk. Pat to last 4 sts. K2tog. K2.

2nd row: Work even in pat.**

Rep last 2 rows 21 (27-32) times more. Leave rem 55 (57-61) sts on a st holder.

FRONT

Rep from ** to ** as given for Back.

Rep last 2 rows 14 (20-25) times more. 69 (71-75) sts.

SHAPE NECK

1st row: (RS) K2. ssk. Pat across 11 sts (neck edge). Turn. Leave rem sts on a spare needle. 14 sts rem.

2nd row: Work 2tog. Pat to end of row. 13 sts.

3rd row: K2. ssk. Pat to last 2 sts. Work 2tog. 11 sts.

4th row: As 2nd row.

5th row: As 3rd row. 8 sts.

6th row: Work even in pat.

7th row: As 3rd row. 6 sts.

8th row: Work even in pat.

9th row: K2. ssk. Work 2tog. 4 sts.

10th row: Work even in pat.

11th row: K2. ssk. 3 sts.

12th row: P3.

13th row: K1. ssk. 2 sts.

14th row: P2togtbl.

Fasten off.

With RS facing, slip next 39 (41-45) sts onto a st holder. Pat to last 4 sts. K2tog. K2. 14 sts rem.

2nd row: Pat to last 2 sts. Work 2tog. 13 sts.

3rd row: Work 2tog. Pat to last 4 sts. K2tog. K2. 11 sts.

4th row: As 2nd row. 10 sts.

5th row: As 3rd row. 8 sts.

6th row: Work even in pat.

7th row: As 3rd row. 6 sts.

8th row: Work even in pat.

9th row: Work 2tog. K2tog. K2. 4 sts.

10th row: Work even in pat.

11th row: K2tog. K2. 3 sts.

12th row: P3.

13th row: K2tog. K1. 2 sts.

14th row: P2tog.

Fasten off.

SLEEVES

With pair of needles, cast on 90 (96-99) sts.

1st row: (RS) K2. *P2. K1tbl. Rep from * to last 4 sts. P2. K2.

2nd row: P2. *K2. P1tbl. Rep from * to last 4 sts. K2. P2.

Rep last 2 rows of Rib Pat for 1½"/4cm, ending on a WS row. PM at each end of last row.

SHAPE RAGLANS

Keeping cont of Rib Pat, proceed as follows:

1st row: (RS) K2. ssk. Pat to last 4 sts. K2tog. K2.

2nd row: P3. Pat to last 3 sts. P3.

3rd row: K3. Pat to last 2 sts. K3.

4th row: As 2nd row.

Rep last 4 rows 29 (31-33) times more. 30 (32-31) sts. Proceed as follows:

1st row: (RS) K2. ssk. Pat to last 4 sts. K2tog. K2.

2nd row: P3. Pat to last 3 sts. P3. Rep last 2 rows 9 (9-8) times more. Leave rem 10 (12-13) sts on a st holder.

FINISHING

BACK LOWER EDGING

With circular needle, beg at marker, pick up and knit 72 (76-80) sts down left back curve, 47 (60-73) sts across cast on edge and 72 (76-80) sts up right back curve. 191 (212-233) sts.

1st row: (WS) *K2. P1tbl. Rep from * to last 2 sts. K2.

2nd row: *P2. K1tbl. Rep from * to last 2 sts. P2.

Rep last 2 rows of (K1tbl. P2) ribbing for 1½"/4cm, ending on a WS row.

Cast off.

BATWING SWONCHO

Rep for Front Lower Edging. Sew raglan seams, matching markers, leaving left back seam open.

COLLAR

With RS facing and circular needle, K10 (12-13) from left sleeve st holder. Pick up and knit 18 sts down left front neck edge. K39 (41-45) from front st holder. Pick up and knit 18 sts up right front neck edge, K10 (12-13) from right sleeve st holder and K53 (57-61) from back st holder, dec 2 (0-1) st(s) at center. 146 (158-167) sts. Do not join.

Work back and forth across needle in rows as follows:

1st row: (WS) Knit.

2nd row: Purl.

3rd row: *K2. P1tbl. Rep from * to last 2 sts. K2.

4th row: *P2. K1tbl. Rep from * to last 2 sts. P2.

Rep 3rd and 4th rows for (K1tbl. P2) ribbing for 7"/18cm, ending on a RS row.

SEW SEAMS

Cast off in pat. Sew back left raglan seam and Collar seam, reversing 4"/10cm for turn back. Sew seams of sleeves from cast on edge to markers (1½"/4cm). •

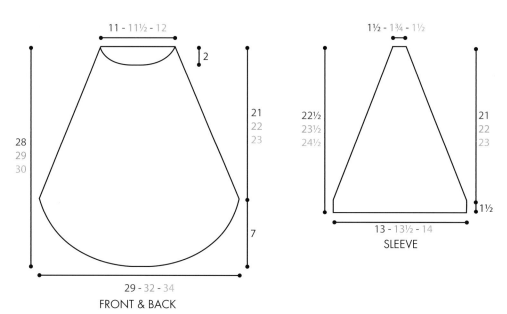

FRONT & BACK

SLEEVE

Key

☐ = Knit on RS rows. Purl on WS rows

⊟ = Purl on RS rows. Knit on WS rows

𝟈 = K1tbl

⚹ = P1tbl

◣ = ssk

◺ = K2tog

◉ = yo

Start Here

BIG RIB COWL

MEASUREMENTS

Approx 36"/91.5cm x 19"/48cm

MATERIALS

YARN

Bernat® Softee® Chunky™, 3½oz/100g balls, each approx 108yd/99m (acrylic)

• 2 balls in #28046 Grey Heather

NEEDLES

• One size 13 (9mm) circular needle, 24"/60cm long, *or size needed to obtain gauge*

GAUGE

10 sts and 14 rows = 4"/10cm using size 13 (9mm) needle in St st. *TAKE TIME TO CHECK GAUGE.*

COWL

Cast on 58 sts. Twist sts once to form mobius loop. Join to work in rnd, placing marker on first st.

1st rnd: (RS) Knit.

2nd rnd: *K1below. P1. Rep from * around.

3rd rnd: *K1. P1below. Rep from * around.

Rep last 2 rnds until work from beg measures 19"/48cm, ending with 3rd rnd.

Next rnd: Knit.

Cast off.

Fold Cowl in half. •

EASY EYELET STITCH WRAP

Basic

MEASUREMENTS

Approx 24"/61cm x 70"/178cm

MATERIALS

YARN

Patons® Alpaca Blend™, 3½oz/100g balls, each approx 155yd/142m (acrylic, wool, nylon, alpaca) 5

• 7 balls in #01010 Iceberg

NEEDLES

• One size 10 (6mm) circular needle, 29"/73.5cm long, *or size needed to obtain gauge*

GAUGE

15 sts and 30 rows = 4"/10cm using size 10 (6mm) needle in Easy Eyelet Pat. *TAKE TIME TO CHECK GAUGE.*

NOTE

Wrap is reversible. There is no right or wrong side.

WRAP

Cast on 91 sts (multiple of 3 sts + 16). Do not join. Working back and forth across needle in rows, proceed as follows:

Knit 16 rows (garter st).

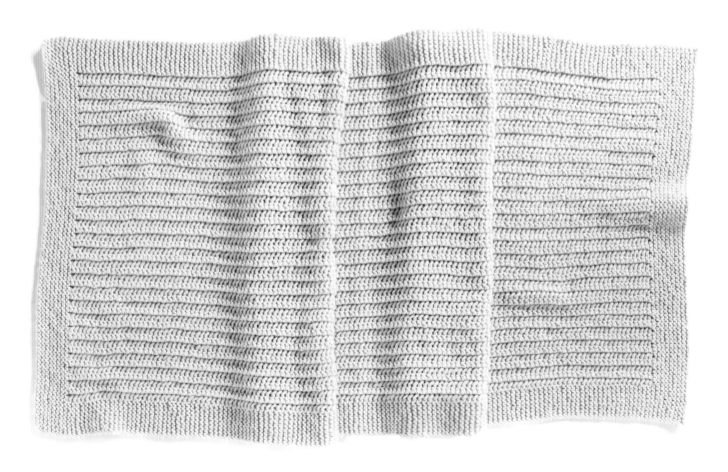

Next row: Knit 8 (K8). *K1. Yarn over (yo). Knit next 2 sts together (K2tog). Repeat (Rep) from * to last 8 sts. K8.

Rep last row for Easy Eyelet Pat until work from beginning (beg) measures 68"/173cm.

Knit 16 rows (garter st).

Cast off.

FINISHING

Pin Wrap to measurements on a flat surface. Cover with a damp cloth, leaving cloth to dry. •

1 Start here

Key

☐ = Knit

⊡ = yo

⊿ = K2tog

COZY SET

MEASUREMENTS

MITTENS AND HAT

One size to fit average woman.

SCARF

Approx 7/18cm x 70/178cm

MATERIALS

YARN

Bernat® Roving™, 3½oz/100g balls, each approx 120yd/109m (acrylic, wool)

• 3 balls in #00103 Lazuli

NEEDLES

• One set (4) double-pointed needles (dpn) size 10½ (6.5mm), *or size needed to obtain gauge*
• One pair size 11 (8mm) knitting needles, *or size needed to obtain gauge*

GAUGE

MITTENS

12 sts and 16 rows = 4"/10cm using size 10½ (6.5mm) needles in St st.

HAT AND SCARF

11 sts and 15 rows = 4"/10cm using size 11 (8mm) needles in St st. *TAKE TIME TO CHECK GAUGE.*

STITCH GLOSSARY

C2B Knit into back of 2nd st on left-hand needle, then knit first stitch, slipping both stitches off needle at same time.

C2P Purl into front of 2nd st on left-hand needle, then purl first stitch, slipping both stitches off needle at same time.

SCARF

Cast on 28 sts.

1st row: (RS) K1. *C2B. K2. Rep from * to last 3 sts. C2B. K1.

2nd row: K1. *P2. K2. Rep from * to last 3 sts. P2. K1.

Rep last 2 rows for pat until Scarf measures 70"/178cm, ending with a WS row.

Cast off.

HAT

Cast on 64 sts.

1st row: (RS) K1. *C2B. K2. Rep from * to last 3 sts. C2B. K1.

2nd row: K1. *P2. K2. Rep from * to last 3 sts. P2. K1.

Rep last 2 rows for pat until work from beg measures 3"/7.5cm, ending with a 2nd row.

Note: At this point, WS becomes RS and RS becomes WS for cuff turnback.

Next row: As 2nd row.

Next row: As 1st row.

Rep last 2 rows for pat until work from beg measures 8"/20.5cm, ending with a WS row.

SHAPE TOP

1st row: (RS) K1. *C2B. K2. C2B. K2tog. Rep from * to last 7 sts. C2B. K2. C2B. K1. 57 sts.

2nd row: K1. P2. *K2. P2. K1. P2. Rep from * to last 5 sts. K2. P2. K1.

3rd row: K1. *C2B. K2tog. C2B. K1. Rep from * to last 7 sts. C2B. K2tog. C2B. K1. 49 sts.

4th row: K1. *P2. K1. Rep from * to last 3 sts. P2. K1.

5th row: K1. *(C2B. K1) twice. K2tog. K1. Rep from * to last 3 sts. C2B. K1. 44 sts.

6th row: K1. P2. K3. *(P2. K1) twice. K2. Rep from * to last 6 sts. (P2. K1) twice.

7th row: K1. *C2B. K1. K2tog. K3. Rep from * to last 3 sts. C2B. K1. 39 sts.

8th row: K1. *P2. K5. Rep from * to last 3 sts. P2. K1.

9th row: K1. *C2B. K1. K2tog. K2. Rep from * to last 3 sts. C2B. K1. 34 sts.

10th row: K1. *P2. K2tog. K2. Rep from * to last 3 sts.

P2. K1. 29 sts.

11th row: K1. *C2B. K2tog. K1. Rep from * to last 3 sts. C2B. K1. 24 sts.

12th row: K1. *P2. K2tog. Rep from * to last 3 sts. P2. K1. 19 sts.

13th row: K1. *K1. K2tog. Rep from * to end of row. 13 sts.

COZY SET

FINISHING

Break yarn, leaving a long end. Thread end through rem sts and tighten securely. Sew back seam, reversing bottom 3"/7.5cm for turn back.

MITTEN (MAKE 2)

With set of four double-pointed needles, cast on 24 sts. Divide sts on 3 needles. Join in rnd. Mark first st with contrast thread.

1st rnd: *K2. P2. Rep from * around.

Rep last rnd of (K2. P2) ribbing for 2 ins [5cm, inc 4 sts evenly across last rnd. 28 sts.

Proceed in pat as follows:

1st rnd: *C2B. K2. Rep from * around.

2nd rnd: *K2. P2. Rep from * around.

Rep last 2 rnds of pat twice more.

SHAPE THUMB GUSSET

1st rnd: Pat 14 sts. M1. Pat to end of rnd.

2nd rnd: Pat 14 sts. P1. Pat to end of rnd.

3rd rnd: Pat 14 sts. M1. K1. M1. Pat to end of rnd.

4th rnd: Pat 14 sts. P3. Pat to end of rnd.

5th rnd: Pat 14 sts. M1. K3. M1. Pat to end of rnd.

6th rnd: Pat 14 sts. P5. Pat to end of rnd.

7th rnd: Pat 14 sts. M1. K5. M1. Pat to end of rnd.

8th rnd: Pat 14 sts. P7. Pat to end of rnd.

9th rnd: Pat 14 sts. Slip next 7 sts onto safety pin (thumb opening). Pat to end of rnd. 28 sts.

Pat in rnds until work from beg measures 8½"/21.5cm, ending with 2nd rnd of pat.

SHAPE TOP

1st rnd: *C2B. K2tog. Rep from * around. 18 sts rem.

2nd rnd: *K1. P2tog. Rep from * around. 12 sts rem.

3rd rnd: *P2tog. Rep from * around. 6 sts rem. Break yarn, leaving a long end. Thread end through rem sts and tighten securely.

THUMB

K7 from safety pin. Pick up and knit 1 st at base of thumb. Divide these 8 sts onto 3 needles.

Next rnd: Purl.

Next rnd: Knit. Rep last 2 rnds until work from pick up rnd measures 2 ins [5cm, ending with a purl rnd.

Next rnd: (K2tog) 4 times. 4 sts rem.

FINISHING

Break yarn, leaving a long end. Thread end through rem sts and tighten securely. •

COMFY EASY EYELET STITCH COCOON

Basic

SIZES

To fit bust measurement:

XS/S/M: 28–34"/71–86.5cm

L/XL/2XL: 40–48"/101.5–122cm

3/4/5XL: 54–62"/137–157.5cm

MATERIALS

YARN

Red Heart® *Super Saver*®, 7oz/198g balls, each approx 364yd/215m (acrylic) **4**

• 3 (3, 4) balls in Country Blue (0382)

NEEDLES

• One size 9 (5.5mm) circular needle, 29"/73.5cm long, *or size needed to obtain gauge*

• One size 10 (6mm) circular needle, 29"/73.5cm long, *or size needed to obtain gauge*

NOTIONS

• Stitch markers

• Yarn needle

GAUGE

12 sts and 24 rows = 4"/10cm with larger needles in pat. *TAKE TIME TO CHECK GAUGE.*

NOTES

The instructions are written for smallest size. If changes are necessary for larger size(s) the instructions will be written thus ( ). When only one number is given, it applies to all sizes.

BODY

Note: Garment is worked in one piece. Cuffs are worked in finishing.

COMFY EASY EYELET STITCH COCOON

With smaller circular needle, cast on 155 (163-171) stitches (sts). Do not join.

Working back and forth across needle, proceed as follows:

1st row: (RS). Knit 1 (K1). *Purl 1 (P1). K1. Repeat (Rep) from * to end of row.

2nd row: P1. *K1. P1. Rep from * to end of row.

Rep these 2 rows (K1. P1) ribbing for 1½"/4cm, ending on a Wrong Side (WS) row and increasing (inc) 1 (decreasing (dec) 1-0) st at center of last row. 156 (162-171) sts.

Change to larger circular needle and proceed in pattern (pat) as follows:

1st row: (RS) *K1. yarn over (yo). Knit next 2 sts together (K2tog). Rep from * to end of row.

Rep last row for pat until work from beg measures 37½ (39½-41½)"/95 (100.5-105.5)cm, ending on a WS row.

Next row: (RS) Knit, dec 1 (Inc 1-0) st at center of last row. 155 (163-171) sts.

With smaller circular needle, work in (K1. P1) ribbing for 1½"/4cm, ending on a WS row.

Cast off in ribbing.

FINISHING

ASSEMBLY

Following diagram, fold work in half, having cast on and cast o¬ff edges at front opening. Place markers 8"/20.5cm, down from fold at each side.

CUFFS

With smaller circular needle, pick up and knit 73 sts between markers. Work in (K1. P1) ribbing as given for Body for 1"/2.5cm, ending on a WS row. Cast off in ribbing. Sew side edges of Garment and Cuffs. •

| ↗ | ⊙ | ☐ | 1 Start here |

Key

☐ = Knit

⊙ = yo

↗ = K2tog

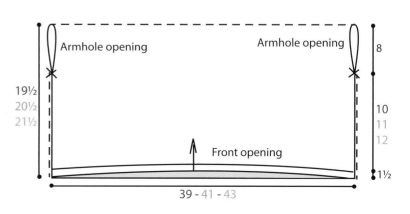

GREAT CURVES PONCHO

Intermediate

SIZES

To fit bust measurement:
XS/S: 28–34"/71–86.5cm
L/XL: 40–46"/101.5–117cm
2/5XL: 48–62"/122–157.5cm

MATERIALS

YARN

Red Heart® Heart Wave™, 3½oz/100g balls, each approx 164yd/150m (acrylic) (4)

• 6 (8, 10) balls in #0420 Radio

NEEDLES

• One pair size 7 (4.5mm) knitting needles, *or size needed to obtain gauge*

• One size 7 (4.5mm) circular needle, 16"/40.5cm long, *or size needed to obtain gauge*

• One size 7 (4.5mm) circular needle, 29"/74cm long, *or size needed to obtain gauge*

NOTIONS

• 4 stitch holders
• Stitch markers

GAUGE

19 sts and 25 rows = 4"/10cm using size 7 (4.5mm) needles in St st. *TAKE TIME TO CHECK GAUGE.*

NOTES

The instructions are written for smallest size. If changes are necessary for larger size(s) the instructions will be written thus ( ). When only one number is given, it applies to all sizes.

DIAMOND PANEL PAT (WORKED OVER 4 STS) (SEE CHART ON PAGE 29)

1st row: (RS) (K1. P1) twice.

2nd and alt rows: Knit all knit sts, purl all purl sts as they appear.

3rd row: P1. K3.

5th row: As 1st row.

7th row: K2. P1. K1.

8th row: As 2nd row.

These 8 rows form Diamond Panel Pat.

BACK AND FRONT (MAKE ALIKE)

With pair of needles, cast on 29 (37-45) sts.

1st row: (RS) Work 1st row of Diamond Panel Pat to last st, noting 4-st rep will be worked 7 (9-11) times. K1.

2nd row: P1. Work 2nd row of Diamond Panel Pat to end of row.

Diamond Panel Pat is now in position.

SHAPE SIDES

Keeping cont of pat, cast on 4 sts at beg of next 10 rows to 69 (77-85) sts, then inc 1 st each end of needle on next 14 rows, taking inc sts into pat. 97 (105-113) sts.

Inc 1 st each end of needle on next and every following alt row 8 times more, taking inc sts into pat, ending on a RS row. 115 (123-131) sts.

Work 3 rows even.

Inc 1 st each end of next and every following 4th row twice more, taking inc sts into pat and ending on a RS row. 121 (129-137) sts.

Work 3 rows even. PM at each end of last row.

SHAPE RAGLANS

Keeping cont of pat, proceed as follows:

1st row: (RS) K2. ssk. Pat to last 4 sts. K2tog. K2.

2nd row: P3. Pat to last 3 sts. P3.

3rd rows: K3. Pat to last 3 sts. K3.

4th row: As 2nd row.

Rep last 4 rows 14 times more. 91 (99-107) sts.

Proceed as follows:

1st row: (RS) K2. ssk. Pat to last 4 sts. K2tog. K2.

2nd row: P3. Pat to last 3 sts. P3.

Rep last 2 rows 25 times more. Leave rem 39 (47-55) sts on a st holder.

LOWER RIBBING

With RS facing and longer circular needle, pick up and knit 155 (163-171) sts along lower edge between markers. Do not join.

Working back and forth across needle in rows, proceed as follows:

1st row: (WS) P1. *K1. P1. Rep from * to end of row.

2nd row: K1. *P1. K1. Rep from * to end of row.

Rep last 2 rows of (K1. P1) ribbing 4 times more, then 1st row once.

Cast off in ribbing.

SLEEVES

With pair of needles, cast on 41 (41-47) sts.

1st row: (RS) K1. *P1. K1. Rep from * to end of row.

2nd row: P1. *K1. P1. Rep from * to end of row.

Rep last 2 rows of (K1. P1) ribbing until work from beg measures 4"/10cm, ending on a RS row. PM at each end of last row.

Next row: (WS) *P1. (P1. K1) in next st. Rep from * to last 1 (1-3) st(s). P1 (1-3) sts. 61 (61-69) sts.

Proceed as follows:

1st row: (RS) Work 1st row of Diamond Panel Pat to last st, noting 4-st rep will be worked 15 (15-17) times. K1.

GREAT CURVES PONCHO

2nd row: P1. Work 2nd row of Diamond Panel Pat to end of row. Diamond Panel Pat is now in position. Keeping cont of pat, inc 1 st each end of needle on next and every following alt row 10 times more to 83 (83-91) sts, then every following 4th row 3 times more, taking inc sts into pat and ending on a RS row. 89 (89-97) sts.

Work 3 rows even.

SHAPE RAGLANS

Keeping cont of pat, cast off 5 sts beg next 2 rows. 79 (79-87) sts.

1st row: (RS) K2. ssk. Pat to last 4 sts. K2tog. K2.

2nd row: P3. Pat to last 3 sts. P3.

3rd rows: K3. Pat to last 3 sts. K3.

4th row: As 2nd row.

Rep last 4 rows 25 times more. 27 (27-35) sts.

Proceed as follows:

1st row: (RS) K2. ssk. Pat to last 4 sts. K2tog. K2.

2nd row: P3. Pat to last 3 sts. P3.

Rep last 2 rows 3 times more. Leave rem 19 (19-27) sts on a st holder.

FINISHING

Pin all pieces to measurements. Cover with a damp cloth leaving cloth to dry. Sew Sleeve seams. Overlap Lower Ribbing at underarm and sew sides tog. Sew raglan and underarm seams.

NECKBAND

With RS facing and shorter circular needle, beg at back left raglan seam, K19 (19-27) from Left Sleeve st holder. K39 (47-55) sts from Front st holder. K19 (19-27) from Right Sleeve st holder. K39 (47-55) sts from Back st holder. 116 (132-164) sts.

Join in rnd. PM on first st.

1st rnd: *K1. P1. Rep from * around.

Rep last rnd 4 times more.

Cast off in ribbing. •

Chart

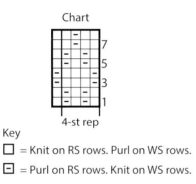

4-st rep

Key

☐ = Knit on RS rows. Purl on WS rows.

⊟ = Purl on RS rows. Knit on WS rows.

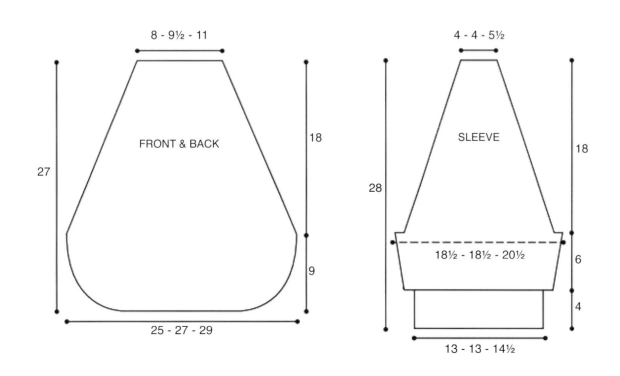

MINIMALIST JACKET

SIZES

To fit bust measurement:

XS/S: 28–34"/71–86.5cm

M: 36–38"/91.5–96.5cm

L: 40–42"/101.5–106.5cm

XL: 44–46"/112–117cm

2/3XL: 48–54"/122–137cm

4/5XL: 56–62"/142–157.5cm

MATERIALS

YARN

Bernat®Softee® Chunky™, 3½oz/100g balls, each
approx 108yd/99m (acrylic) **6**

• 10 (11, 12, 13, 14, 15) balls in #28219 Seagreen

NEEDLES

• One size 11(8mm) circular needle, 40"/101.5cm long,
or size needed to obtain gauge

NOTIONS

• Spare needle
• Stitch marker

GAUGE

10 sts and 28 rows = 4"/10cm using size 11 (8mm)
needle in garter st. *TAKE TIME TO CHECK GAUGE.*

NOTES

The instructions are written for smallest size. If changes
are necessary for larger size(s) the instructions will be
written thus ( ). When only one number is given, it
applies to all sizes.

JACKET

Note: Jacket is worked sideways in one piece from cuff
to cuff.

Beg at Left Sleeve, cast on 4 sts.

Work i-cord cast on as follows:

1st row: Knit. Slip 4 sts just knit back onto lefthand
needle.

2nd row: Inc 1 st in first st. Knit to end of row. Slip 4 sts
just knit back onto lefthand needle. (1 st increased). Rep
last row until there are 44 (44-48-48-50-52) sts.

Next row: Slip last 3 sts just knit back onto left-hand
needle. K2tog. K1. Slip last 2 sts back onto left-hand
needle. K2tog. 42 (42-46-46-48-50) sts.

Cont in garter st (knit every row), noting first row is WS
until work from beg measures 8½ (8-8-7¼-7-6¼)"/21.5
(20.5-20.5-18.5-18-16)cm, ending on a WS row.

SHAPE BACK AND FRONT

Cast on 60 (60-62-62-64-64) sts at beg of next 2 rows.
162 (162-170-170-176-178) sts.

Cont even in garter st until work from last cast on row
measures 7½ (8½-9¼-10¼-11-12)"/19 (21.5-23.5-26-
28-30.5) cm, ending on a WS row.

DIVIDE FOR NECK

1st row: (RS) K78 (78-82-82-85-86) and place on spare
needle for Back. Cast off 8 sts for neck. Knit to end of
row. 76 (76-80-80-83-84) sts. Knit 9 rows even.

SHAPE LEFT NECK

Next row: (RS) K2. ssk. Knit to end of row. Knit 5 rows
even.

Next row: K2. ssk. Knit to end of row. Knit 3 rows even.

Next row: K2. ssk. Knit to end of row. Rep last 4 rows once more.

Next row: Knit.

SIZES 2/3XL AND 4/5XL ONLY:

Next row: K2. ssk. Knit to end of row.

Next row: Knit.

ALL SIZES:

Next row: (RS) K2. ssk. Knit to end of row.

Next row: Knit to last 4 sts. K2tog. K2.

Rep last 2 rows 0 (0-1-1-1-1) time more.

Cast off rem 70 (70-72-72-74-75) sts. With WS facing, join yarn to 78 (78-82-82-85-86) sts on spare needle for Back.

Cont in garter st until work from join measures 7 (7-7½-7½-8-8)"/18 (18-19-19-20.5-20.5) cm, ending on a RS row. Place sts on spare needle.

RIGHT FRONT

Cast on 70 (70-72-72-74-75) sts.

SHAPE RIGHT NECK

Next row: (RS) K2. M1. Knit to end of row.

Next row: Knit to last 2 sts. M1. K1. Rep last 2 rows 0 (0-1-1-1-1) time more. 72 (72-76-76-78-79) sts.

Sizes 2/3XL and 4/5XL only:

Next row: K2. M1. Knit to end of row.

Next row: Knit.

ALL SIZES:

Next row: (RS) K2. M1. Knit to end of row.

Knit 3 rows even.

Next row: K2. M1. Knit to end of row.

Rep last 4 rows once more.

Knit 5 rows even.

Next row: K2. M1. Knit to end of row. 76 (76-80-80-83-84) sts.

Knit 10 rows even.

MINIMALIST JACKET

JOIN BACK AND FRONT

Next row: (WS) K76 (76-80-80-83-84). Cast on 8 sts. K78 (78-82-82-85-86) across Back sts from spare needle. 162 (162-170-170-176-178) sts. Place marker at end of last row.

Cont in garter st until work from marker measures 7½ (8½-9¼-10¼-11-12)"/19 (21.5-23.5-26-26-30.5)cm, ending on a RS row.

DIVIDE FOR RIGHT SLEEVE

Cast off 60 (60-62-62-64-64) sts at beg of next 2 rows. 42 (42-48-48-48-50) sts.

Cont in garter st until Right Sleeve measures 8½ (8-8-7¼-7-6¼)"/21.5 (20.5-20.5-18.5-18-16)cm, ending on a RS row.

I-CORD CAST-OFF

Cast on 3 sts onto end of left-hand needle. *K2. K2tog. Slip last 3 sts back onto left-hand needle. Rep from * until 3 sts rem. K2tog. K1. Slip last 2 sts onto end of left-hand needle. K2tog. Fasten off.

FINISHING

Sew side and underarm seams.

APPLIED I-CORD EDGING

With RS facing, beg at Left Front, pick up and knit 110 (120-130-140-150-160) sts along bottom edge of Jacket. Break yarn. Cast on 2 sts. K2, then knit first picked up st on bottom edge. Slip last 3 sts onto left-hand needle. *K2. K2togtbl. Slip last 3 sts onto left-hand needle. Rep from * until 3 sts rem. K2tog. K1. Slip last 2 sts onto end of left-hand needle. K2tog. Fasten off.

With RS facing and beg at bottom Right Front, pick up and knit 88 (88-92-92-95-97) sts up Right Front edge to neck shaping, 62 (62-68-68-74-74) sts to beg of Left Front neck shaping and 88 (88-92-92-95-97) sts down Left Front edge. 238 (238-252-252-264-268) sts. Break yarn. Cast on 2 sts. K2, then knit first picked up st on Right Front. Slip last 3 sts onto left-hand needle. *K2. K2togtbl. Slip last 3 sts onto left-hand needle. Rep from * until 3 sts rem. K2tog. K1. Slip last 2 sts onto end of left-hand needle. K2tog.

Fasten off. •

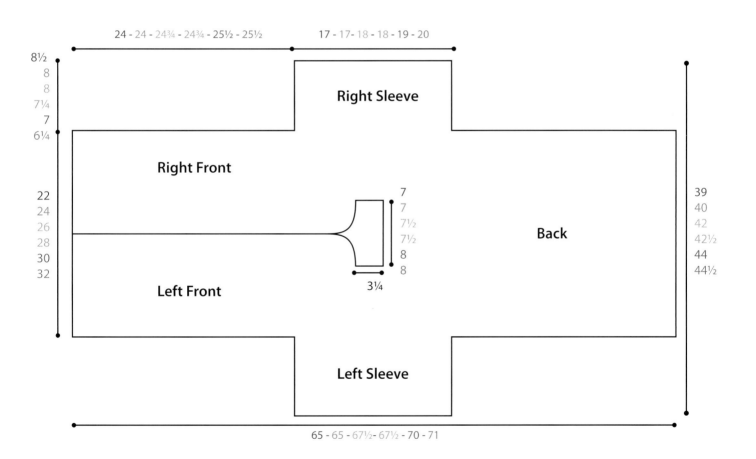

SLOUCHY SWEATER DRESS

Intermediate

SIZES

To fit bust measurement:

XS/S: 28–34"/71–86.5cm

M: 36–38"/91.5–96.5cm

L: 40–42"/101.5–106.5cm

XL: 44–46"/112–117cm

2/3XL: 48–54"/122–137cm

4/5XL: 56–62"/142–157.5cm

MATERIALS

YARN

Bernat® Roving™, 3½oz/100g balls, each approx 120yd/109m (acrylic, wool) (5)

• 7 (7, 8, 9, 10, 11) balls #00032 Putty (MC)

YARN

Bernat® Satin™, 3½oz/100g balls, each approx 200yd/182m (acrylic) (4)

• 1 ball in #04045 Grey Mist Heather (A)

NEEDLES

• One pair size 7 (4.5mm) knitting needles, *or size needed to obtain gauge*

• One pair size 10½ (6.5mm) knitting needles, *or size needed to obtain gauge*

• One pair size 11 (8mm) knitting needles, *or size needed to obtain gauge*

NOTIONS

• 4 stitch holders

• 2 stitch markers

GAUGE

11 sts and 15 rows = 4"/10cm using size 11 (8mm) needles and MC in St st. *TAKE TIME TO CHECK GAUGE.*

NOTES

The instructions are written for smallest size. If changes are necessary for larger size(s) the instructions will be written thus ( ). When only one number is given, it applies to all sizes.

FRONT

**With MC and U.S. 10½ (6.5 mm) needles, cast on 66 (70-78-82-94-102) sts.

1st row: (RS) *K2. P2. Rep from * to last 2 sts. K2.

2nd row: *P2. K2. Rep from * to last 2 sts. P2.

Rep last 2 rows for (K2. P2) ribbing for 3"/7.5cm, ending on a WS row and dec 3 sts on last row. 63 (67-75-79-91-99) sts.

Change to U.S. 11 (8 mm) needles and proceed in Basket Rib Pat as follows:

1st row: (RS) Knit.

2nd row: Purl.

3rd row: *K1. Sl1Pwyib. Rep from * to last st. K1.

4th row: *K1. Sl1Pwyif. Rep from * to last st. K1. Last 4 rows form Basket Rib Pat.**

Cont in pat until work from beg measures 6 (6-7-7-8-8)"/15 (15-18-18-20.5-20.5)cm, ending on a WS row.

Next row: K1. ssk. Pat to last 3 sts. K2tog. K1. Work 7 rows in pat.

Keeping cont of pat, dec 1 st each end of needle every 10th row 4 (4-5-4-6-5) times more. 53 (57-63-69-77-87) sts.**

AT THE SAME TIME, when work from beg measures approx 16 (16-17-18-19-20)"/40.5 (40.5-43-45.5-48-51)cm, ending on a 4th row, divide and work Pockets as follows:

PLACE POCKETS

Next row: K9 (9-9-10-10-10). Place last 9 (9-9-10-10-

10) sts on a st holder. (Kfb) 3 times. Knit to last 12 (12-12-13-13-13) sts. (Kfb) 3 times. Turn. Leave rem sts on st holder.

Working on these sts, cont as follows:

1st row: (WS) (P1. K1) 3 times. Pat to last 6 sts. (K1. P1) 3 times.

2nd row: (K1. P1) 3 times. Pat to last 6 sts. (P1. K1) 3 times.

Rep last 2 rows 7 times more, then 1st row once.

Next row: (RS) (K2tog) 3 times. Pat to last 6 sts. (K2tog) 3 times. Leave sts on spare needle.

LEFT SIDE

With WS facing and MC, pick up and knit 1 st in each purl "bump" of the (K1. P1) ribbing of Front. Pat across 9 (9-9-10-10-10) sts from st holder. 12 (12-12-13-13-13) sts.

1st row: (RS) Pat to last 3 sts. K1. P1. K1.

2nd row: P1. K1. P1. Pat to end of row.

Rep last 2 rows 5 times more, keeping cont of side dec as before. Leave sts on st holder.

RIGHT SIDE

With RS facing and MC, pick up and knit 1 st in each purl "bump" of (K1. P1) ribbing of Front on WS of work. Pat across 9 (9-9-10-10-10) sts from st holder.

1st row: (WS) Pat to last 3 sts. P1. K1. P1.

2nd row: K1. P1. K1. Pat to end of row.

Rep last 2 rows 5 times more, then 1st row once, keeping cont of side dec as before. Leave sts on st holder.

JOIN SIDES AND CENTER FRONT

Next row: (RS) Join yarn to Left Side. Pat across 9 (9-9-10-10-10) sts. Align needles, holding last 3 sts on needle behind first 3 sts of Front, K3, knitting through both thicknesses at once. Pat to last 3 sts. Align needles, holding sts of Right Side behind Front, K3, knitting through both thicknesses at once. Pat to end of row.

Keeping cont of Basket Rib Pat, and side dec every 10th row from previous dec to 53 (57-63-69-77-87) sts, work until Front from beg measures 26 (26-28-30-32-32)"/66 (66-71-76-81.5-81.5)cm, ending on a WS row.

SLOUCHY SWEATER DRESS

SHAPE RAGLANS

Keeping cont of pat, cast off 2 (2-2-3-3-3) sts beg next 2 rows. 49 (53-59-63-71-81) sts.

1st row: (RS) K1. ssk. Pat to last 3 sts. K2tog. K1. 47 (51-57-61-69-79) sts.

2nd row: P2. Pat to last 2 sts. P2. Dec 1 st each end of needle on next and every following alt row 6 (7-7-5-4-0) times more. 33 (35-41-49-59-77) sts.

Purl 1 row.

SIZES L, XL, 2/3XL AND 4/5XL ONLY:

Dec 1 st each end of needle on next (2-4-8-16) rows. (37-41-43-45) sts.

SIZE XS/S, M AND L ONLY:
SHAPE NECK

1st row: K1. ssk. Pat across next 7 sts. K2tog. Turn. Leave rem sts on spare needle.

2nd row: Pat to last 3 sts. P2togtbl. P1.

3rd row: K1. ssk. Pat to last 2 sts. K2tog.

4th row: Pat to last 3 sts. P2togtbl. P1.

5th row: As 3rd row.

6th row: P1. P2togtbl. P1.

7th row: K1. K2tog.

8th row: P2tog.

Fasten off.

With RS facing, slip next 9 (11-13) sts onto a st holder. Join yarn to rem sts and proceed as follows:

1st row: ssk. Pat to last 3 sts. K2tog. K1.

2nd row: P1. P2tog. Pat to end of row.

3rd and 4th rows: As 1st and 2nd rows.

5th row: ssk. K1. K2tog. K1.

6th row: P1. P2tog. P1.

7th row: K2tog. K1.

8th row: P2tog.

Fasten off.

SIZES XL, 2/3XL AND 4/5XL ONLY:
SHAPE NECK

1st row: K1. ssk. Pat across next 9 sts. K2tog. Turn. Leave rem sts on spare needle.

2nd row: Pat to last 3 sts. P2togtbl. P1.

3rd row: K1. ssk. Pat to last 2 sts. K2tog.

4th and 5th rows: As 2nd and 3rd rows.

6th row: As 2nd row.

7th row: K1. ssk. K2tog.

8th row: P1. P2tog.

9th row: K2tog.

Fasten off.

With RS facing, slip next (13-15-17) sts onto a st holder. Join yarn to rem sts and proceed as follows:

1st row: ssk. Pat to last 3 sts. K2tog. K1.

2nd row: P1. P2tog. Pat to end of row.

3rd–6th rows: As 1st and 2nd rows twice.

7th row: ssk. K2tog. K1.

8th row: P2tog. P1.

9th row: K2tog.

Fasten off.

BACK

Work from ** to ** as given for Front.

Cont even in Basket Rib Pat until work from beg measures 26 (26-28-30-32-32)"/66 (66-71-76-81.5-81.5)cm, ending on a WS row.

SHAPE RAGLANS

Keeping cont of pat, cast off 2 (2-2-3-3-3) sts beg next 2 rows. 49 (53-59-63-71-81) sts.

1st row: (RS) K1. ssk. Pat to last 3 sts. K2tog. K1. 47 (51-57-61-69-79) sts.

2nd row: P2. Pat to last 2 sts. P2. Dec 1 st each end of needle next and every following alt row 7 (7-7-5-4-0) times more. 31 (35-41-49-59-77) sts.

Purl 1 row.

Dec 1 st each end of needle every row to 21 (21-23-23-25-25) sts. Leave these 21 (21-23-23-25-25) sts on a st holder.

SLEEVES

With MC and U.S. 101/2 (6.5 mm) needles, cast on 30 (30-30-34-34-34) sts.

1st row: (RS) *K2. P2. Rep from * to last 2 sts. K2.

2nd row: *P2. K2. Rep from * to last 2 sts. P2. Rep last 2 rows for (K2. P2) ribbing for 1½"/4cm, ending on a WS row, and inc 1 st in center of last row. 31 (31-31-35-35-35) sts.

Change to larger needles and proceed in Basket Rib Pat as follows:

1st row: (RS) Knit.

2nd row: Purl.

3rd row: *K1. Sl1Pwyib. Rep from * to last st. K1.

4th row: *K1. Sl1Pwyif. Rep from * to last st. K1. Last 4 rows form Basket Rib Pat.

Keeping cont of pat, inc 1 st each end of needle on next and every 10th (8th-6th6th-6th-4th) row 3 (4-4-3-3-3) times, taking inc sts into pat. 39 (41-41-41-41-41) sts.

SIZES L, XL, 2/3XL AND 4/5XL ONLY:

Inc 1 st each end of needle every following (8th-8th-8th-6th) row (1-2-2-4) time(s) more, taking inc sts into pat. (43-45-45-49) sts.

ALL SIZES

Cont even in pat until work from beg measures 14½ (14½-14½-15½ -15½-15½)"/37 (37-37-39-39-39)cm, ending on a WS row.

SHAPE RAGLANS

Keeping cont of pat, cast off 2 (2-2-3-3-3) sts beg next 2 rows. 35 (37-39-39-39-43) sts.

1st row: (RS) K1. ssk. Pat to last 3 sts. K2tog. K1. 33 (35-37-37-37-41) sts.

2nd row: P2. Pat to last 2 sts. P2. Dec 1 st each end of needle next and every following alt row 5 (6-8-10-10-8) times more. 21 (21-21-19-15-23) sts.

Purl 1 row.

Dec 1 st each end of needle every row to 7 (7-7-9-9-9) sts. Leave these 7 (7-7-9-9-9) sts on a st holder.

FINISHING

Pin pieces to measurements. Cover with a damp cloth leaving cloth to dry. Sew raglan seams leaving back raglan seam open.

Note: To reduce bulk, use Bernat® SatinT™ for seaming.

COLLAR

With RS facing, MC and U.S. 10½ (6.5 mm) needles, K7 (7-7-9-9-9) from Left Sleeve st holder. Pick up and knit 9 (9-9-10-10-10) sts down left front neck edge. K9 (11-13-13-15-17) from Front st holder. Pick up and knit 9 (9-9-10-10-10) sts up right front neck edge. K7 (7-7-9-9-9) from Right Sleeve st holder. K21 (21-23-23-25-25) from Back st holder, inc 0 (2-2-0-0-2) sts evenly across. 62 (66-70-74-78-82) sts.

1st row: *K2. P2. Rep from * to last 2 sts. K2.

2nd row: *P2. K2. Rep from * to last 2 sts. P2.

SLOUCHY SWEATER DRESS

Rep last 2 rows of (K2. P2) ribbing until Collar measures 4"/10cm.

Change to U.S. 11 (8 mm) needles and cont in (K2. P2) ribbing until Collar measures 8"/20.5cm from beg, ending on a WS row.

Next row: (RS) *K1. M1. K1. P2. Rep from * to last 2 sts. K1. M1. K1. 78 (83-88-93-98-103) sts.

Next row: *P3. K2. Rep from * to last 3 sts. P3.

Next row: *K3. P2. Rep from * to last 3 sts. K3.

Rep last 2 rows until Collar measures 12"/30.5cm. Cast off loosely in pat. Sew left back raglan and Collar seam.

LEFT POCKET LINING

With A and U.S. 7 (4.5 mm) needles, cast on 12 sts. With WS facing, pick up and knit 24 sts along Left Side pocket opening. 36 sts.

**1st row: (WS) K3. Purl to last 3 sts. K3.

2nd row: Knit. Rep last 2 rows until Pocket Lining measures 7"/18cm, ending on a WS row.

Cast off loosely. Sew 3 side edges to WS of work, being careful to not sew through to RS of work.**

RIGHT POCKET LINING

With RS facing, A and U.S. 7 (4.5 mm) needles, pick up and knit 24 sts along Right Side pocket opening. Cast on 12 sts. 36 sts. Work from ** to ** as given for Left Pocket Lining.

SEW SEAMS

Sew side and sleeve seams. •

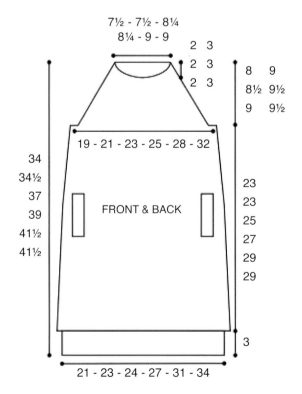

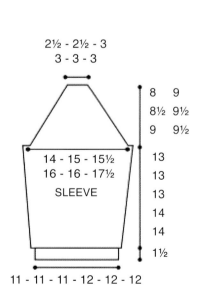

MOBIUS COWL

Easy

MEASUREMENTS

Approx 36"/91.5cm x 19"/48cm

MATERIALS

YARN

Bernat® Roving™, 3½oz/100g balls, each approx 120yd/109m (acrylic, wool) **5**

• 2 balls in #00033 Flint

NEEDLES

• One size 13 (9mm) circular needle, 24"/60cm long, *or size needed to obtain gauge*

GAUGE

10 sts and 14 rows = 4"/10cm using size 13 (9mm) needle in St st. *TAKE TIME TO CHECK GAUGE.*

COWL

Cast on 58 sts. Twist sts once to form mobius loop. Join to work in rnd, placing marker on first st.

1st rnd: (RS) Knit.

2nd rnd: *K1below. P1. Rep from * around.

3rd rnd: *K1. P1below. Rep from * around.

Rep last 2 rnds until piece from beg measures 19"/48cm, ending with 3rd rnd .

Next rnd: Knit.

Cast off. Fold Cowl in half. •

HONEYCOMB TWIST SUPER SCARF

Intermediate

MEASUREMENTS

Approx 10"/25.5cm x 110"/279.5cm, excluding fringe

MATERIALS

YARN

Patons® Classic Wool Roving™, 3½oz/100g balls, each approx 120yd/109m (wool) **5**

• 7 balls in #77420 Pale Blush or #77615 Yellow or #77008 Aran

NEEDLES

• One pair size 10 (6mm) knitting needles, *or size needed to obtain gauge*

GAUGE

15 sts and 20 rows = 4"/10cm using size 10 (6mm) needles in St st. *TAKE TIME TO CHECK GAUGE.*

STITCH GLOSSARY

C2B Slip next stitch onto cable needle and leave at back of work. K1, then K1 from cable needle.

C2F Slip next stitch onto cable needle and leave at front of front. K1, then K1 from cable needle.

C6B Slip next 3 stitches onto cable needle and leave at back of work. K3, then K3 from cable needle.

C6F Slip next 3 stitches onto cable needle and leave at front of work. K3, then K3 from cable needle.

C14B Slip next 7 stitches onto cable needle and leave at back of work. K6. P1 then (P1. K6) from cable needle.

C14F Slip next 7 stitches onto cable needle and leave at front of work. K6. P1 then (P1. K6) from cable needle.

SCARF

Cast on 36 sts.

Knit 3 rows (garter st), noting first row is RS.

Next row: (WS) K3. (Kfb. K2) 10 times. K3. 46 sts.

Beg Cable pat as follows: (See chart on page 42.)

1st row: (RS) (K6. P2) twice. K1tbl. (C2B. C2F) 3 times. K1tbl. (P2. K6) twice.

2nd and alt rows: (P6. K2) twice. P1tbl. P12. P1tbl. (K2. P6) twice.

3rd row: (K6. P2) twice. K1tbl. (C2F. C2B) 3 times. K1tbl. (P2. K6) twice.

5th row: As 1st row.

7th rows: C6B. P2. K6. P2. K1tbl. (C2F. C2B) 3 times. K1tbl. P2. K6. P2. C6F.

9th to 30th rows: As 1st through 8th rows twice more, then rep 1st to 6th rows once.

31st row: C14B. P2. K1tbl. (C2F. C2B) 3 times. K1tbl. P2. C14F.

32nd row: (P6. K2) twice. P1tbl. P12. P1tbl. (K2. P6) twice.

These 32 rows form Cable Pat.

HONEYCOMB TWIST SUPER SCARF

Cont in Cable Pat until work from beg measures approx 110"/279.5cm, ending on a 29th row.

Next row: (WS) K3. (K2tog. K2) 10 times. K3. 36 sts.

Knit 3 rows (garter st).

Cast off.

FINISHING

FRINGE

Cut strands of yarn 16"/40.5cm long. Taking 2 strands tog, fold in half and knot into fringe across ends of Scarf. Trim fringe evenly. •

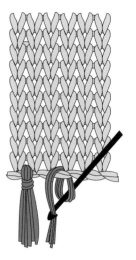

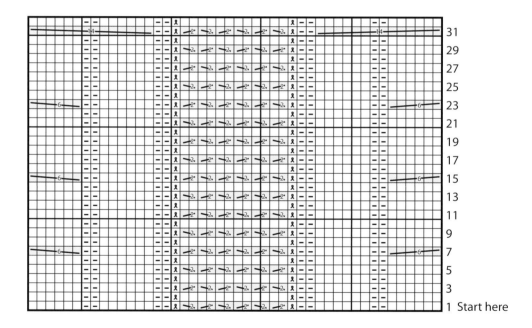

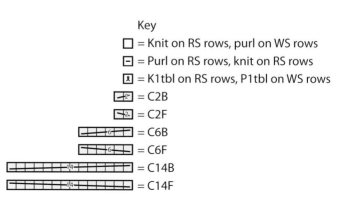

Key

☐ = Knit on RS rows, purl on WS rows

⊟ = Purl on RS rows, knit on RS rows

⚡ = K1tbl on RS rows, P1tbl on WS rows

◪ = C2B

◪ = C2F

▭ = C6B

▭ = C6F

▭ = C14B

▭ = C14F

VINTAGE SWEATER SCARF

Easy

MEASUREMENTS

Approx 20"/51cm x 62"/157.5cm

MATERIALS

YARN

Red Heart® *With Love*®, 7oz/198g balls, each approx 370yd/338m (acrylic) **4**

• 3 balls in Pewter (1401)

NEEDLES

• One pair size 8 (5mm) knitting needles, *or size needed to obtain gauge*
• One pair size 9 (5.5mm) knitting needles, *or size needed to obtain gauge*

NOTIONS

• Tape measure
• Stitch markers
• Four ⁷⁄₈"/22mm buttons
• Yarn needle

GAUGE

14 sts = 4"/10cm with size 8 (5mm) needles in Garter stitch (knit every row). *TAKE TIME TO CHECK GAUGE.*

NOTES

• Sweater Scarf is made from a rectangle and a thin belt.
• The rectangle is worked back and forth in rows in three sections: Left front rib section, Center Garter stitch section, and right front rib section.
• The belt is sewn to the center of the long, lower edge of the rectangle (see diagram on page 44).

SWEATER SCARF

With larger needles, cast on 70 sts.

LEFT FRONT RIB SECTION

1st row: (RS) K4 for Garter st border, place marker, p2, *kfb, p2; repeat from * to last 4 sts, place marker, k4 for Garter st border—90 sts.

2nd row: (WS) K4, slip marker, k2, *p2tog, k2; repeat from * to next marker, slip marker, k4—70 sts.
Repeat 1st and 2nd rows until piece measures about 10"/25.5cm from beginning, end with a wrong side row (Row 2)—70 sts.

CENTER GARTER STITCH SECTION

Change to smaller needles. Continue to slip markers as you come to them.
Work in Garter st (knit every row) until piece measures

VINTAGE SWEATER SCARF

about 52"/132cm from beginning, end with a wrong side row.

RIGHT FRONT RIB SECTION

Change to larger needles.

Repeat 1st and 2nd rows of left front rib section for 3"/7.5cm, end with a wrong side row.

1st Buttonhole row: (RS) K4, slip marker, p2, *kfb, p2; repeat from * to next marker, slip marker, k1, bind off 2 sts for buttonhole—88 sts.

2nd Buttonhole row: (WS) K1, cast on 2 sts, k1, slip marker, k2, *p2tog, k2; repeat from * to next marker, slip marker, k4—70 sts.

Repeat 1st and 2nd rows of left front rib section until piece measures about 3½"/9cm from first buttonhole, end with a wrong side row.

Repeat 1st and 2nd Buttonhole rows.

Repeat 1st and 2nd rows of left front rib section until piece measures about 3½"/9cm from 2nd buttonhole, end with a wrong side row.

Repeat 1st and 2nd Buttonhole rows.

Repeat 1st and 2nd rows of left front rib section until

piece measures about 10"/25.5cm from beginning of right front rib section, end with a wrong side row—70 sts.

Bind off in pattern.

BELT

With tape measure, measure your true waist.

With smaller needles, cast on 8 sts.

Work in Garter st for 3 rows.

1st Buttonhole row: K3, bind off 2 sts, knit to end of row—6 sts.

2nd Buttonhole row: K3, cast on 2 sts, k3— 8 sts.

Work even in Garter st until piece measures same as waist measurement. Bind off.

FINISHING

Fold Sweater Scarf in half and place a marker on long edge.(opposite buttonhole edge) at fold for center. Fold belt in half and place a marker on one edge at fold for center. Sew marked sides of sweater scarf and belt together, beginning at marked center, sewing for about 4"/10cm on each side, and stretching the belt slightly as you sew.

Sew three buttons along left front edge of sweater scarf, opposite buttonholes along right front edge. Sew remaining button to end of belt opposite buttonhole. Weave in all ends. •

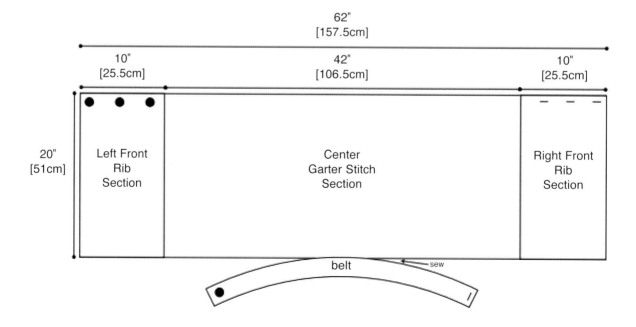

SHOULDER HOODIE

Intermediate

MEASUREMENTS

Circumference at shoulders 34"/86.5cm (unstretched)

MATERIALS

Yarn

Caron® *Simply Soft*®, 6 oz/170g balls, each approx 315yd/288m (acrylic) **4**

• 5 balls in #9756 Lavender Blue

NEEDLES

• One size 15 (10mm) circular needle, 29"/73.5cm long, *or size needed to obtain gauge*

NOTIONS

• Size K/10½ (6.5mm) crochet hook
• Cable needle (cn)
• Stitch marker
• Yarn needle

GAUGE

10 sts = 4"/10cm using using size U.S. 15 (10mm) needle and 3 strands of yarn held together in St st.
TAKE TIME TO CHECK GAUGE.

CABLE PATT (WORKED IN-THE-RND):

1st–4th rnds: *P3, k4; repeat from * around.

5th rnd: *P3, slip 2 sts cable needle (cn), hold in back, k2, then k2 sts from cn; repeat from * around.

6th rnd: *P3, k4; repeat from * around.

Repeat 1st–6th rnds for patt worked in-the-rnd.

CABLE PATT (WORKED BACK AND FORTH):

1st and 3rd rows: (RS) *P3, k4; repeat from * across.

2nd and 4th rows: (WS) *P4, k3; repeat from * across.

5th row: *P3, slip 2 sts cable needle (cn), hold in back, k2, then k2 sts from cn; repeat from * across.

6th row: *P4, k3; repeat from * across.

Repeat 1st–6th rows for patt worked back and forth.

NOTES

Hoodie is knitted in one piece to neck opening. Stitches are then bound off for opening and work is continued by knitting back and forth in rows.

HOODIE

Using 3 strands of yarn held together, CO 105 sts. Join, being careful not to twist sts. Place marker to indicate beg of rnd.

1st–4th rnds: *P3, k4; repeat from * around.

5th rnd: *P3, slip 2 sts cable needle (cn), hold in back, k2, then k2 sts from cn; repeat from * around.

6th rnd: *P3, k4; repeat from * around.

Repeat 1st through 6th rnds for patt until piece measures 13"/33cm from CO edge, ending with patt 6th rnd.

Remove marker then work back and forth as follows:

Next row: (RS) P2, working in patt as established BO next 34 sts, work to end of row—71 sts.

Work remaining sts back and forth in rows in patt as established until piece measures 27"/69cm from CO edge.

BO all sts in patt.

FINISHING

Fold hood in half and sew top seam. Using yarn needle, weave in all loose ends. Block if necessary, being careful not to stretch out cables.

TIE

Using 3 strands of yarn held together and crochet hook, make a chain 50"/127cm long. Weave tie through sts at approximately 9"/23cm up from bottom edge. •

WRAPOVER SWONCHO

SIZES

To fit bust measurement:

XS/S/M: 28–38"/71–96.5cm

L/XL/2XL 40–48"/101.5–122cm

3/4/5XL 54–62"/137–157.5cm

MATERIALS

YARN

Patons® Classic Wool Worsted™, 3½oz/100g balls, each approx 194yd/177m (wool)

• 9 (11, 13) balls in #00225 Dark Gray Mix

NEEDLES

• One size 6 (4mm) circular needle, 16"/40.5cm long, *or size needed to obtain gauge*

• One size 6 (4mm) circular needle, 32"/81.5cm long, *or size needed to obtain gauge*

• One size 6 (4mm) circular needle, 40"/101.5cm long, *or size needed to obtain gauge*

• One size 7 (4.5mm) circular needle, 32"/81.5cm long, *or size needed to obtain gauge*

NOTIONS

• 2 spare needles of similar size

• Stitch holder

• 4 stitch markers

GAUGE

21 sts and 30 rows = 4"/10cm with larger needles in Shaker Rib pat. *TAKE TIME TO CHECK GAUGE.*

NOTES

The instructions are written for smallest size. If changes are necessary for larger size(s) the instructions will be written thus ( ). When only one number is given, it applies to all sizes.

BACK

With smaller, longer circular needle, cast on 204 (216-228)sts. Do not join.

Working back and forth in rows, proceed as follows:

1st row: (RS) Sl1. *K1tbl. P1. Rep from * to last st. K1.

2nd row: Sl1. *K1. P1. Rep from * to last st. P1.

Rep last 2 rows ribbing twice more, then first row once.

Next row: (WS) K13 (7-13). *K2tog. K5 (6-6). Rep from * to last 9 (1-7) sts. Knit to end of row. 178 (190-202) sts.

Change to larger, longer needle and proceed in Shaker Rib Pat as follows:

1st row: (RS) Sl1. P2. *K1below. P2. Rep from * to last st. P1.

2nd row: Sl1. Knit to end of row.

Rep last 2 rows for Shaker Rib Pat until work from beg measures 18½ (20-21)"/47 (51-53.5)cm, ending on a WS row.

SHAPE SHOULDERS

1st row: (RS) Sl1. P2. K1below. ssk. Pat to last 6 sts. K2tog. K1below. P3.

2nd row: Sl1. Knit to end of row.

Rep last 2 rows 8 (8-9) times more. 160 (172-182) sts.

Next row: (RS) Sl1. P2. K1below. (ssk) twice. Pat to last 8 sts. (K2tog) twice. K1below. P3.

Next row: Sl1. Knit to end of row.

Rep last 2 rows 26 (28-30) times more. 52 (56-58) sts. Leave sts on st holder.

LEFT FRONT

**With smaller, longer circular needle, cast on 114 (120-126)sts. Do not join.

Working back and forth in rows, proceed as follows:

1st row: (RS) Sl1. *K1tbl. P1. Rep from * to last st. K1.

2nd row: Sl1. *K1. P1. Rep from * to last st. P1.

WRAPOVER SWONCHO

Rep last 2 rows ribbing twice more, then first row once.**

Next row: (WS) Sl1. (K1. P1) 3 times. K5 (1-4). *K5 (6-6). K2tog. Rep from * to last 4 (0-3) sts. K4 (0-3). 100 (106-112) sts.

Change to larger, longer circular needle and proceed as follows:

1st row: (RS) Sl1. P2. *K1below. P2. Rep from * to last 7 sts. K1. (P1. K1tbl) 3 times.

2nd row: Sl1. (K1. P1) 3 times. Knit to end of row.

Rep last 2 rows until work from beg measures 11½ (14-16)"/29 (35.5-40.5)cm, ending on a WS row.

SHAPE SHOULDER

1st row: (RS) Sl1. P2. K1below. ssk. Pat to last 7 sts. K1. (P1. K1tbl) 3 times.

2nd row: Sl1. (K1. P1) 3 times. Knit to end of row.

Rep last 2 rows 8 (8-9) times more. 91 (97-102) sts.

Next row: (RS) Sl1. P2. K1below. (ssk) twice. Pat to last 7 sts. K1. (P1. K1tbl) 3 times.

Next row: Sl1. (K1. P1) 3 times. Knit to end of row.

Next row: Sl1. P2. K1below. (ssk) twice. Pat to last 7 sts. K1. (P1. K1tbl) 3 times.

Rep last 2 rows 16 (18-20) times more. 55 (57-58) sts.

SHAPE NECK

1st row: (WS) Sl1. (K1. P1) 3 times. K21 (23-24). Slip these last 28 (30-31) sts onto spare needle. Knit to end of row. 27 sts.

2nd row: (RS) P3. K1below. (ssk) twice. Pat to last 3 sts. P2tog. P1.

3rd row: Knit.

Rep last 2 rows 5 times more. 9 sts.

Next row: (RS) P3. ssk. P3tog. P1. 6 sts.

Next row: Knit.

Next row: P1. Sl1. P3tog. psso. P1. 3 sts.

Next row: Sl1. P2tog. psso. 1 st.

Fasten off.

RIGHT FRONT

Work from ** to ** as given for Left Front.

Next row: (WS) K4 (0-3). *K5 (6-6). K2tog. Rep from * to last 12 (8-11) sts. K5 (1-4). P1. (K1. P1) 3 times. 100 (106-112)sts.

Change to larger, longer circular needle and proceed as follows:

1st row: (RS) Sl1. (P1. K1tbl) 3 times. *P2. K1below. Rep from * to last 3 sts. P3.

2nd row: Sl1. Knit to last 7 sts. P1. (K1. P1) 3 times.

Rep last 2 rows until work from beg measures 8½ (11-13)"/21.5 (28-33)cm, ending on a WS row.

SHAPE SHOULDER

1st row: (RS) Sl1. (P1. K1tbl) 3 times. *P2. K1below. Rep from * to last 6 sts. K2tog. K1below. P3.

2nd row: Sl1. Knit to last 7 sts. P1. (K1. P1) 3 times.

Rep last 2 rows 8 (8-9) times more. 91 (97-102) sts.

Next row: (RS) Sl1. (P1. K1tbl) 3 times. *P2. K1below. Rep from * to last 8 sts. (K2tog) twice. K1below. P3.

WRAPOVER SWONCHO

Next row: Sl1. Knit to last 7 sts. P1. (K1. P1) 3 times.
Rep last 2 rows 16 (18-20) times more. 57 (59-60) sts.

SHAPE NECK

1st row: (RS) BREAK YARN. Slip first 28 (30-31) sts
onto spare needle. WITH NEW STRAND OF YARN. Pat to
last 8 sts. (K2tog) twice. K1below. P3. 27 sts.
2nd row: Knit.

3rd row: P1. P2tog. Pat to last 8 sts. (K2tog) twice.
K1below. P3. 4th row: Knit.
Rep last 2 rows 5 times more. 9 sts.
Next row: (RS) P1. P3tog. K2tog. P3. 6 sts.
Next row: Knit. **Next row:** P1. Sl1. P3tog. psso. P1. 3 sts.
Next row: Sl1. P2tog. psso. 1 st.
Fasten off.

SLEEVES

With smaller, shorter circular needle, cast on 56 (58-60)
sts. Do not join.
Working back and forth in rows, proceed as follows:

ROLLED EDGE

1st to 3rd rows: Knit.
4th row: (WS) Purl.
5th row: Knit.
6th row: Purl. Rep last 2 rows once more.
Cast off.
With smaller, shorter circular needle, pick up and knit
56 (58-60) sts at WS of Rolled Edge using garter ridge
at cast on as a guide.
1st row: (RS) K1. *K1tbl. P1. Rep from * to last st. K1.
2nd row: P1. *K1. P1. Rep from * to last st. P1.
Rep last 2 rows ribbing until work from beg measures
12"/30.5cm, ending on a RS row.
Cast off in ribbing (WS).

FINISHING

Sew shoulder seams. Overlap Right Front over Left
Front, aligning sts on spare needles. Place markers
5 (5¼-5½)"/12.5 (13.5-14)cm down from shoulder
seams at each side edge. Sew in sleeves between
markers. Sew side and sleeve seams.

NECK EDGING

With smaller, shorter circular needle, RS facing and beg
at left shoulder seam, pick up and knit 12 sts down Left
Front neck edge. Working sts from Right Front spare
needle tog with aligned sts from Left Front spare needle
AT SAME TIME, K28 (30-31). Pick up and knit 12 sts up
Right Front neck edge. K52 (56-58) from Back neck st
holder. Join in rnd, placing marker for beg of rnd. 104
(110-113) sts.

ROLLED EDGE

Knit 5 rnds. Cast off.

RIBBED COLLAR

With smaller, shorter circular needle, pick up and knit 104 (108-112) sts at base of Rolled Edge at WS, using ridge from neckline pick up as a guide (rolled edge is in front of Ribbed Collar—see photo).

1st rnd: *K2. P2. Rep from * around.

Rep last rnd until Ribbed collar measures 10"/25.5cm.

Cast off in ribbing. •

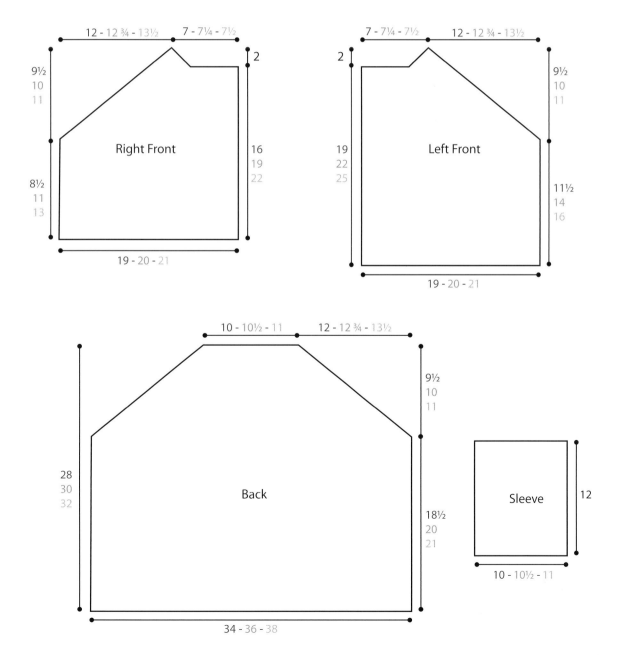

LONG WEEKEND CARDIGAN

Easy

SIZES

To fit bust measurement:

XS/S: 28–34"/71–86.5cm

M: 36–38"/91.5–96.5cm

L: 40–42"/101.5–106.5cm

XL: 44–46"/112–117cm

2/3XL: 48–54"/122–137cm

4/5XL: 56–62"/142–157.5cm

MATERIALS

YARN

Patons® Classic Wool Worsted™, 3½oz/100g balls, each approx 194yd/177m (wool)

Long Version

• 9 (9, 10, 10, 11, 12) balls in #77307 Plum Heather

Hip Length Version

• 8 (9, 9, 10, 10, 11) balls in #00224 Grey Mix

Short Version

• 6 (6, 7, 7, 8, 8) balls in #77118 Blue Heather

NEEDLES

• One pair size 7 (4.5mm) knitting needles, *or size needed to obtain gauge*

• One pair size 9 (5.5mm) knitting needles, *or size needed to obtain gauge*

NOTIONS

• 6 stitch markers

• Yarn needle

GAUGE

20 sts and 32 rows = 4"/10cm iwith larger needles in Basket Rib pat. *TAKE TIME TO CHECK GAUGE.*

NOTES

The instructions are written for smallest size. If changes are necessary for larger size(s) the instructions will be written thus ( ). When only one number is given, it applies to all sizes.

BACK

With smaller needles, cast on 100 (112-124-136-148-160) sts.

1st row: (RS) *K4. P2. Rep from * to last 4 sts. K4.

2nd row: *P4. K2. Rep from * to last 4 sts. P4.

Rep last 2 rows of (K4. P2) ribbing until work from beg measures 5"/12.5cm, ending on a WS row and inc (dec-dec-inc-dec-inc) 1 (1-3-1-1-1) sts in center of last row. 101 (111-121-137-147-161) sts.

Change to larger needles and proceed in Basket Rib Pat as follows:

1st row: (RS) Knit.

2nd row: Purl.

3rd row: *K1. Sl1P. Rep from * to last st. K1.

4th row: *K1. Sl1Pwyif. Rep from * to last st. K1.

These 4 rows form Basket Rib Pat.

LONG VERSION ONLY:

Cont in pat until work from beg measures 34 (34-35-35-37-37)"/86.5 (86.5-89-89-94-94)cm, ending on a WS row.

HIP LENGTH VERSION ONLY:

Cont in pat until work from beg measures 28 (28-29-29-31-31)"/71 (71-73.5-73.5-78.5-78.5)cm, ending on a WS row.

SHORT VERSION ONLY:

Cont in pat until work from beg measures 19 (19-20-20-22-22)"/48 (48-51-51-56-56)cm, ending on a WS row.

ALL VERSIONS:

SHAPE SHOULDERS

Keeping cont of pat, cast off 10 (10-12-12-13-15) sts beg next 4 rows, then 7 (9-9-11-12-14) sts beg following 4 rows. Cast off rem 33 (35-37-45-47-45) sts.

RIGHT FRONT

**With smaller needles, cast on 46 (52-58-64-70-76) sts.

Work 5"/12.5cm in (K4. P2) ribbing as given for Back, ending on a WS row and inc 1 st in center of last row. 47 (53-59-65-71-77) sts.

Change to larger needles and proceed in Basket Rib Pat as given for Back.

LONG WEEKEND CARDIGAN

LONG VERSION ONLY:

Cont in pat until work from beg measures 25 (24½-25-25-26½-26)"/63.5 (62-63.5-63.5-67.5-66)cm, ending on a WS row.**

HIP LENGTH VERSION ONLY:

Cont in pat until work from beg measures 19 (18½-19-19-20½-20)"/48 (47-48-48-52-51)cm, ending on a WS row.**

SHORT VERSION ONLY:

Cont in pat until work from beg measures 10 (9½-10-10-11½-11)"/25.5(24-25-25-29-28)cm, ending on a WS row.**

ALL VERSIONS
SHAPE NECK

Next row: (RS) K1. ssk (neck edge). Pat to end of row.
Work 5 (5-5-5-3-3) rows even in pat.
Cont in pat, dec 1 st at neck edge on next and every following 6th (6th-6th-6th-4th-4th) row to 37 (43-52-61-52-59) sts, then every following 4th (4th-4th-4th-2nd-2nd) row to 34 (38-42-46-48-58)sts.
Cont even in pat until work from beg measures same length as Back to shoulder, ending on a RS row.

SHAPE SHOULDER

Next row: (WS) Cast off 10 (10-12-12-13-15) sts. Pat to end of row.
Next row: Work even in pat. Rep last 2 rows once more.
Next row: Cast off 7 (9-9-11-11-14) sts. Pat to end of row.
Next row: Work even in pat. Cast off rem 7 (9-9-11-11-14) sts.

LEFT FRONT

Work from ** to ** as given for Right Front.

SHAPE NECK

Next row: (RS) Pat to last 3 sts. K2tog. K1 (neck edge). Work 5 (5-5-5-3-3) rows even in pat.
Cont in pat, dec 1 st at neck edge on next and every following 6th (6th-6th-6th-4th-4th) row to 37 (43-52-61-52-59) sts, then every following 4th (4th-4th-4th2nd-2nd) row to 34 (38-42-46-48-58) sts.
Cont even in pat until work from beg measures same length as Back to shoulder, ending on a WS row.

SHAPE SHOULDER

Next row: (RS) Cast off 10 (10-12-12-13-15) sts. Pat to end of row.
Next row: Work even in pat. Rep last 2 rows once more.
Next row: Cast off 7 (9-9-11-11-14) sts. Pat to end of row.
Next row: Work even in pat.
Cast off rem 7 (9-9-11-11-14) sts.

SLEEVES

With smaller needles, cast on 46 (46-52-52-58-58) sts. Work 4"/10cm in (K4. P2) ribbing as given for Back, ending on a WS row and inc 1 st in center of last row. 47 (47-53-53-59-59) sts.
Change to larger needles and proceed in Basket Rib Pat as given for Back for 2 rows. Inc 1 st each end of next and following 4th (4th-2nd-2nd-2nd2nd) row until there are 91 (95-101-101-105-109) sts, taking inc sts into pat.
Cont even in pat until Sleeve from beg measures 18 (17½-17-17-16-15½)"/45.5 (44.5-43-43-40.5-39.5)cm, ending on a WS row.
Cast off in pat.

POCKETS (MAKE 2) (LONG & HIP LENGTH VERSIONS ONLY)

With larger needles, cast on 31 sts.
Work in Basket Rib Pat as given for Back for 5"/12.5cm,

ending on a WS row and dec 1 st in center of last row. 30 sts.

Next row: (RS) *K2. P2. Rep from * to last 2 sts. K2.

Next row: *P2. K2. Rep from * to last 2 sts. P2.

Rep last 2 rows of (K2. P2) ribbing 6 times more.

Cast off loosely in ribbing.

FINISHING

Pin pieces to measurements. Cover with a damp cloth, leaving cloth to dry. Sew shoulder seams. Place markers on side edges of Back and Fronts 9 (9½-10-10-10½-11)"/23 (24-25.5-25.5-26.5-28)cm down from shoulders. Sew in Sleeves between markers.

LONG & HIP LENGTH VERSIONS ONLY:

Place markers on side edges 5"/12.5cm up from cast on edges. Sew side and sleeve seams to markers. (Leave ribbing open). Sew Pockets to each Front, approx 2"/5cm in from front edge and 3"/7.5cm up from top of ribbing.

SHORT VERSION ONLY:

Sew side and sleeve seams.

FRONT BAND

With smaller needles, cast on 18 sts.

1st row: (RS) K1. (P1. K1) 8 times. K1.

2nd row: (K1. P1) 9 times.

Rep last 2 rows until band, when slightly stretched, measures length to fit up Left Front edge, across back neck edge and down Right Front edge, sewing in place as you work.

Cast off in ribbing. •

LONG WEEKEND CARDIGAN

Long Version:

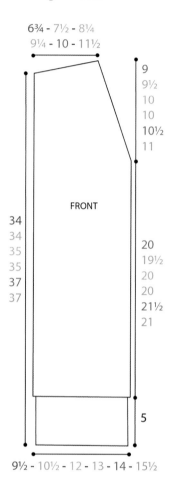

6¾ - 7½ - 8¼
9¼ - 10 - 11½

9
9½
10
10
10½
11

34
34
35
35
37
37

FRONT

20
19½
20
20
21½
21

5

9½ - 10½ - 12 - 13 - 14 - 15½

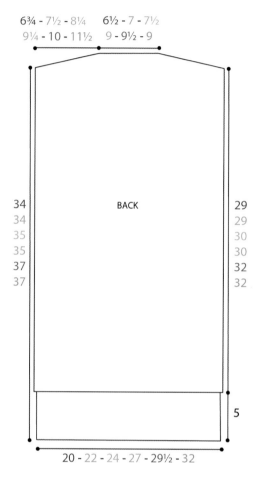

6¾ - 7½ - 8¼   6½ - 7 - 7½
9¼ - 10 - 11½   9 - 9½ - 9

34   29
34   29
35   30
35   30
37   32
37   32

BACK

5

20 - 22 - 24 - 27 - 29½ - 32

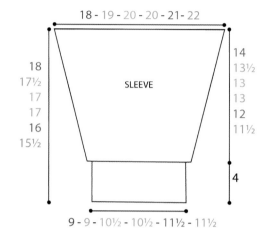

18 - 19 - 20 - 20 - 21 - 22

18
17½
17
17
16
15½

SLEEVE

14
13½
13
13
12
11½

4

9 - 9 - 10½ - 10½ - 11½ - 11½

Hip Length Version:

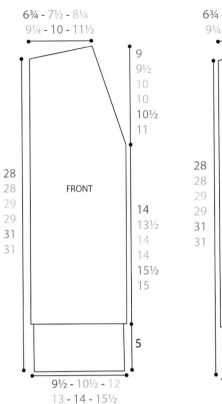

6¾ - 7½ - 8¼
9¼ - 10 - 11½

9
9½
10
10
10½
11

FRONT

28
28
29
29
31
31

14
13½
14
14
15½
15

5

9½ - 10½ - 12
13 - 14 - 15½

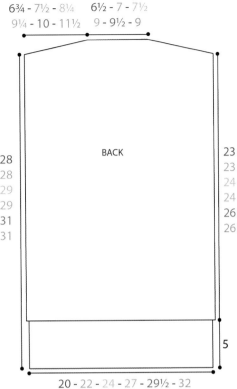

6¾ - 7½ - 8¼   6½ - 7 - 7½
9¼ - 10 - 11½   9 - 9½ - 9

BACK

28
28
29
29
31
31

23
23
24
24
26
26

5

20 - 22 - 24 - 27 - 29½ - 32

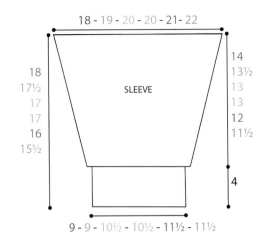

18 - 19 - 20 - 20 - 21- 22

SLEEVE

18
17½
17
17
16
15½

14
13½
13
13
12
11½

4

9 - 9 - 10½ - 10½ - 11½ - 11½

Short Version:

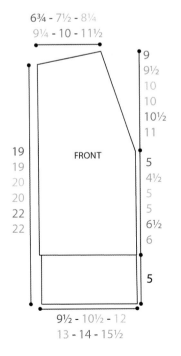

6¾ - 7½ - 8¼
9¼ - 10 - 11½

9
9½
10
10
10½
11

5
4½
5
5
6½
6

FRONT

19
19
20
20
22
22

5

9½ - 10½ - 12
13 - 14 - 15½

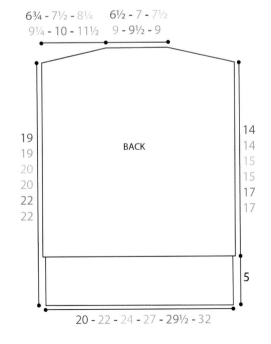

6¾ - 7½ - 8¼   6½ - 7 - 7½
9¼ - 10 - 11½   9 - 9½ - 9

BACK

19
19
20
20
22
22

14
14
15
15
17
17

5

20 - 22 - 24 - 27 - 29½ - 32

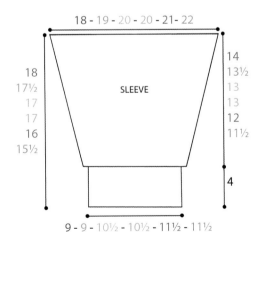

18 - 19 - 20 - 20 - 21- 22

SLEEVE

18
17½
17
17
16
15½

14
13½
13
13
12
11½

4

9 - 9 - 10½ - 10½ - 11½ - 11½

OMBRE ARM WARMERS

Easy

MEASUREMENTS

Wrist Circumference: 6 (7, 8, 9)"/15 (18, 20.5, 23)cm

Upper Arm Circumference: 9 (10, 10½, 12)"/23 (25.5, 26.5, 30.5)cm

Length: 14½ (15½, 16½, 18)"/37 (39.5, 42, 46)cm

MATERIALS

YARN

Red Heart® Super Saver® Ombre™, 10oz/283g balls; each 482yd/440m (acrylic) **④**

• 1 ball in Cocoa (3987)

NEEDLES

• One pair size 8 (5mm) knitting needles, *or size needed to obtain gauge*

NOTION

• Yarn needle

GAUGE

17 sts = 4"/10cm; 23 rows = 4"/10cm in Stockinette stitch. *TAKE TIME TO CHECK GAUGE.*

K2, P2 RIB (MULTIPLE OF 4 STS + 2)

1st row: (WS) [P2, k2] to last 2 sts, p2.

2nd row: [K2, p2] to last 2 sts, k2.

Repeat Rows 1–2 for K2, p2 rib.

ARM WARMERS (MAKE 2)

Cast on 26 (30, 34, 38) sts.

Work in K2, p2 rib for 1½ (2, 2½, 3)"/4 (5, 6, 7.5)cm, end with a wrong side row.

Change to St st and work until piece measures 2¼ (3, 3½, 4¼)"/5.5 (7.5, 9, 11)cm from beginning, end with a wrong side row.

Inc row: (RS) K1, kfb, knit to last 3 sts, kfb, k2—28 (32, 36, 40) sts; 2 sts increased.

Repeat Inc row every 6th row 5 more times—38 (42, 46, 50) sts on last row worked.

Work until piece measures 13 (13½, 14, 15)"/33 (34, 35.5, 38)cm from beginning, end with a wrong side row.

Change to K2, p2 rib and work until piece measures 14½ (15½, 16½, 18)"/37 (39.5, 42, 46)cm, end with a wrong side row.

Bind off.

FINISHING

Sew side seam. If desired, leave 1"/2.5cm unsewn along seam 1"/2.5cm from cast-on edge for thumbhole. Weave in ends. •

SURVIVAL COWL

MEASUREMENTS

Approx 36"/91.5cm, unstretched, around lower edge (above Side Panel)

MATERIALS

YARN

Red Heart® Super Saver® Flecks & Heathers™, 5oz/141g balls, each approx 260yd/238m (acrylic, other fibers)
• 4 balls in Aran Fleck (4313)

NEEDLES

• One size 13 (9mm) circular needle, 32"/80cm long, *or size needed to obtain gauge*

NOTIONS

• One ring stitch marker,
• Detachable stitch markers
• Stitch holder
• Yarn needle

GAUGE

10 sts = 4" (10cm); 14 rows = 4" (10cm) in Small Cable pattern. 12 sts = 4" (10cm); 14 rows = 4" (10cm) in 1x1 Rib. *TAKE TIME TO CHECK GAUGE.*

STITCH GLOSSARY

RT (Right Twist) Knit into the front of the second stitch on the left needle leaving the stitch on the needle, knit the first stitch on the left needle, slipping both stitches off the needle.

1X1 RIB WORKED IN RNDS (OVER EVEN NUMBER OF STS)

1st rnd: (RS) *K1, p1; repeat from * around.
Repeat 1st Rnd for 1x1 Rib.

SMALL CABLE PATTERN (MULTIPLE OF 4 STS + 2)

1st row: (RS): K2, *p2, RT; repeat from * to last 4 sts, p2, k2.

2nd row: Purl.
Repeat last 2 rows for Small Cable pattern.

NOTES

• Cowl is worked in two pieces: Side Panel and Cowl.
• Side Panel is worked back and forth in rows beginning at lower point of panel.
• Cowl is worked in rounds.
• Project is worked with two strands of yarn held together throughout.

SIDE PANEL

With 2 strands of yarn held together, cast on 4 sts. Work back and forth in rows on circular needle as if working with straight needles.

1st row: (RS): Kfb in each st across— 8 sts.

2nd row: Purl.

3rd row: Kfb in each st to last st, k1—15 sts.

4th row: Purl.

5th row: [K1, M1, p1] 7 times, M1, k1—23 sts.

6th row: Purl.

7th row: [K1, kfb, p1] 7 times, k2—30 sts.

8th row: P15, place marker, p15.

9th row: K2, *p2, RT; repeat from * to 1 st before marker, kfb, slip marker, kfb, **RT, p2; repeat from ** to last 2 sts, k2—32 sts.

10th row: Purl, slipping marker as you come to it.

11th row: K2, *p2, RT; repeat from * to 2 sts before marker, p1, kfb, slip marker, kfb, p1, **RT, p2; repeat from ** to last 2 sts, k2— 34 sts.

12th row: Purl, slipping marker as you come to it.

SURVIVAL COWL

13th row: K2, *p2, RT; repeat from * to 3 sts before marker, p2, kfb, slip marker, kfb, p2, **RT, p2; repeat from ** to last 2 sts, k2— 36 sts.

14th row: Purl, slipping marker as you come to it.

15th row: K2, *p2, RT; repeat from * to 4 sts before marker, p2, k1, kfb, slip marker, kfb, k1, p2, **RT, p2; repeat from ** to last 2 sts, k2—38 sts.

16th row: Purl, slipping marker as you come to it.
Repeat Rows 9–16 until there are 76 sts (38 sts on each side of marker), end with a Row 14.

DIVIDE SIDE PANEL INTO TWO HALVES

Next row: (RS) Work Row 1 of Small Cable pattern to marker, remove marker and slip next 38 sts on to a holder.

FIRST HALF

Continue in Small Cable pattern over the remaining 38 sts for 7"/18cm. Bind off.

SECOND HALF

Return 38 sts from stitch holder to needles, ready to work a right side row.
Beginning with Row 1 of pattern, work in Small Cable pattern until second half measures same as first half. Bind off.

COWL

With 2 strands of yarn held together, cast on 108 sts. Join to work in the round, taking care not to twist sts. Work in 1x1 Rib until piece measures about 3" (7.5cm) from beginning.

1st Decrease rnd: [K7, k2tog] 12 times— 96 sts.
Work in 1x1 Rib for 3"/7.5cm for first pleat.

Next rnd: Knit.
Work in 1x1 Rib for 1"/2.5cm.

2nd Decrease rnd: [K6, k2tog] 12 times— 84 sts.
Work in 1x1 Rib for 3"/7.5cm for 2nd pleat.

Next rnd: Knit.

Work in 1x1 Rib for 1"/2.5cm.

3rd Decrease rnd: [K5, k2tog] 12 times— 72 sts.
Work in 1x1 Rib for 3"/7.5cm for 3rd pleat.
Bind off loosely.

FINISHING

Fold each of the Cowl pleats to the outside (right side) and whip stitch the top and bottom of each pleat together on the inside (WS). Using removable stitch markers, attach the two top edges of the Side Panel to the lower edge of the Cowl, leaving 2"/5cm of Cowl between the pieces for the top of armhole, then sew tope edges in place. Weave in all ends. •